# A TERRIBLE
# BEAUTY

An Exploration of the Positive Role of
Violence in Life, Culture and Society

# A TERRIBLE BEAUTY

An Exploration of the Positive Role of
Violence in Life, Culture and Society

## LEON WHITESON

mosaic press

Canadian Cataloguing in Publication Data

Whiteson, Leon, 1930-
A terrible beauty: an exploration of the positive role of violence in life,
culture & society

Includes bibliographical references.
ISBN 0-88962-717-7

1. Violence - Social aspects.  I. Title.

HM1116.W44 2000        303.6        C99-9328794

Published by MOSAIC PRESS, P.O. Box 1032, Oakville, Ontario, L6J 5E9, Canada.
Offices and warehouse at 1252 Speers Road, Units #1&2, Oakville, Ontario, L6L
5N9, Canada and Mosaic Press, 4500 Witmer Industrial Estates, PMB 145, Niagara
Falls, NY 14305-1386

Mosaic Press acknowledges the assistance of the Canada Council, the Ontario Arts
Council and the Department of Canadian Heritage, Government of Canada for
their support of our publishing programme.


**MOSAIC PRESS**, in Canada:
1252 Speers Road, Units #1 & 2,
Oakville, Ontario, L6L 5N9
Phone / Fax: 905-825-2130
ORDERS:
mosaicpress@on.aibn.com
EDITORIAL:
cp507@freenet.toronto.on.ca

**MOSAIC PRESS**, in the USA:
4500 Witmer Industrial Estates
PMB 145, Niagara Falls,
NY 14305-1386  Tel:1-800-387-8992
ORDERS:
mosaicpress@on.aibn.com
EDITORIAL:
cp507@freenet.toronto.on.ca

Le Conseil des Arts      The Canada Council
du Canada       for the Arts

He, too, has resigned his part
In the casual comedy;
He, too, has been changed in his turn,
Transformed utterly:
A terrible beauty is born.

W.B. Yeats,
Easter, 1916

# Other Books by Leon Whiteson

## FICTION

IN THE GARDEN OF DESIRE
Mosaic Press, 2000

WHITE SNAKE
Mosaic Press, 1988

FOOL
Mosaic Press, 1984

NORA ECKDORF
1967

## NON-FICTION

THE LIVEABLE CITY:
THE ARCHITECTURE AND NEIGHBOURHOODS
OF TORONTO
Mosaic Press, 1982

MODERN CANADIAN ARCHITECTURE
1983

THE WATTS TOWERS OF LOS ANGELES
Mosaic Press, 1989

A GARDEN STORY
1995

A PLACE CALLED WACO
1999

# TABLE OF CONTENTS

# INTRODUCTION

Violence is to our age what sex was to the Victorians: a ripe mixture of revulsion and fascination, a threatening energy that is simultaneously repulsive and compelling. For us, violence is a kind of pornography, a vice we roundly condemn and slyly enjoy, a crudely compelling fact of life we seem helpless to confront in any way that makes sense. In truth, we make the same mistake about it that the Victorians did about sex: we treat it as a symptom of moral and cultural pathology, a social disease with no effective cure. We fail to see that violence, like sex, is a valid natural phenomenon with creative as well as destructive possibilities.

Violence is the last true force of nature that still escapes any real attempt at understanding, a vital energy that continues to confound us with its seemingly demonic power. We roundly condemn violence, yet openly enjoy its thrills in movies, TV, comic books, video games and other forms of popular entertainment. We relish ferocious sports such as football and ice hockey, and revel in such gory glories as professional prizefights and wrestling. Unlike our forefathers, who tried to ban any public mention or display of sex, we allow violence a large and open presence in our lives yet remain profoundly ambivalent about its function.

Given the way it captures so much of our attention and concern, it is astonishing that violence is so rarely examined as a primal energy that has played a major role in making us what we are. The psychology of personal and group aggression has been pondered, the role of social conflict has been investigated, and other public and personal interactions which include a strong element of violence have been looked into at length. But violence has rarely been studied on its own terms. "No one engaged in thought about history and politics can remain unaware of the enormous role violence has always played in human affairs," Hannah Arendt wrote, "and it is at first glance rather surprising that violence has been singled out so seldom for special consideration." [1] Having said that, however, Arendt herself failed to follow through with any coherent concept of violence.

It is strange that we're now undaunted by the notion of huge nuclear energies, exploding stars, or even the unimaginable Big Bang with which the universe is said to have begun. We can decipher the genetic code and contemplate the possibilities of genetic engineering. We can begin to penetrate the electro-chemical secrets of the brain, our own three-pound universe. We can study all these things with intense intellectual curiosity; but we seem reluctant to consider the possibility that violence might be a fundamental force with positive as well as negative consequences.

Maybe our minds have been too numbed by the destructive varieties of violence which frequently disrupt and continue to disturb many human events, from the public to the personal. Since 1900, close to 200,000,000 human beings have been killed by their fellows, in wars, in social, ethnic, and political upheavals - and the killing continues. In this century the destructive aspects of violence have been institutionalized as state policy, in nations from the most technologically advanced to the least developed; from the concentration camps of Nazi Germany and the Soviet gulag to the killing fields of Cambodia and Bosnia. In the United States thousands are murdered every year, and many thousands more are victims of one form or another of violent crime and abuse. Around the world, in the heart of the family itself, varieties of violence are rampant.

As we push out into space to probe Jupiter and beyond, as computers proliferate and communications networks contract the Global Village, violence remains the most feared and least understood of all the elements that move and shape us. It has replaced the old theological concept of an abstract Evil driving the dark nature of mankind, the modern version of original sin no savior can appear to redeem.

In a desperate search for understanding, some concerned commentators claim that violence is generated by poverty and abuse. Others hold that it is an evolutionary holdover, a relic of impulses and mental structures man has inherited from primitive ancestors. According to this view, the pace of scientific and technological advance has speeded up so rapidly it has left natural man panting in the rear, fiercely resentful at being outpaced. For yet others, the contemporary fact of violence is an indication that the censor of moral reason is once again asleep, creating a condition Plato graphically described in *The Republic*, in which the wild beast that lurks within gorges at will.

The blunt fact is that the conventional diagnoses show us no real way forward. However valid they may be, they are too limited to offer us any truly useful way to think about violence as a phenomenon rather than a pathology. No current view of violence, whether psychological, biological or sociological, has yet presented us with a point of view that would enable us to grapple with the ferocities that fire our genes. Consequently, our blindly negative perspective on violence has blocked our comprehension and bound us into despair, leaving us stranded between strident cries for censorship, shouts for more prisons, appeals for more clinics, or calls for palliatives to ease the impact of harsh economic realities that are difficult to ameliorate.

Fortunately, we are not condemned to suck on the dry bones of our present arid attitudes; we have a far more nourishing resource to draw upon concerning the role of violence in human affairs. We possess a long inheritance of knowledge and experience that teaches us about the positive purposes of violence in our history. The richness of this heritage, expressed in our sacred rituals and in our arts, offers us a way to begin thinking about violence with some hope of understanding.

We may start by recognizing that the dynamic potential of violence has, throughout history, energized every aspect of our existence, provoking humanity into a wide range of imaginative responses that refine the raw ore of violence into a rich cultural currency, along the way accomplishing many bold spiritual, aesthetic and cultural transformations.

Such transformations illuminate Van Gogh's turbulent last canvases and Mozart's haunted *Don Giovanni*; they animate the fabulous structures architecture has devised in answer to the threat of attack, such as Granada's Alhambra, the walled towns of Tuscany, the Great Wall of China; they metamorphose a brutal act into the powerful image of redemption played out in the Christian Crucifixion and the spectacle of King Oedipus's bloody eyes. In the same transforming mode we have Yeats's rendering of Zeus, disguised as a swan, "the brute blood of the air," [2] locked in the act of raping Leda; a violation that sparked the conception of Helen of Troy and began European history.

Nietzsche urged us to examine the lives of our most creative ancestors, and ask "whether a tree, if it is to grow proudly into the sky, can do without bad weather and storms." Such storms, he suggested, are among "the *favoring* circumstances without which a great increase even in virtue is hardly possible." (Nietzsche's italics.) [3]

What cannot be denied is that these dangerously confused times cry out for a clear way of thinking about the positive as well as the negative capabilities of violence. Rather than condemning violence out of hand as an inherently evil phenomenon, I suggest we might refine our options and attempt to make a subtle and sophisticated discrimination between its creative and destructive possibilities, beginning with an acceptance of violence as a force of nature, a basic condition of existence, an integral aspect of the human experience. Instead of indulging in endlessly futile attempts to dam up the torrents of this natural current, we might strive to recognize and remember its potentially positive purposes, and invent the kind of fresh and resourceful responses to its challenges our forefathers achieved. We might consider relearning old wisdoms we seem to have misplaced, looking back into the history of the human soul, made manifest in our arts and our culture, our doubts and our faith, for ways to rediscover the true significance of violence as a primal energy that moves the natural world and every person in it.

Violence, like sexuality, is an aspect of the vigorous Freudian id galloping along under the reins of the ego of our social and personal will. Comparing the id and the ego to a horse and its rider, Freud declared that the rider has "the prerogative of determining the goal and of guiding the movements of his powerful mount toward it." But, he added, there are times when "the rider is obliged to guide his horse in the direction in which it itself wants to go." [4]

In the ancient Cretan ceremony of bull-leaping, for instance, the leaper did not so much guide the powerful beast as much as manipulate it. If a bull-leaper fumbled and was gored, his gracelessness implied that Minoan society had failed to validate its highest aspirations. On the other hand, if he succeeded, it signified that the animal's potency had been led along a life-enhancing path.

The radical challenge violence offers is aptly described by the poet, Ted Hughes: "Any form of violence...invokes the bigger energy, the elemental power circuit of the Universe...If you refuse the energy, you are living a kind of death. If you accept the energy, it destroys you. What is the alternative? To accept the energy, and find methods of turning it to good..." [5]

In his poem, "Lineage," Hughes succinctly outlines this process of transformation:

> *In the beginning was Scream*
> *Who begat Blood...*
> *Who begat Adam*
> *Who begat Mary*
> *Who begat God...* [6]

\*   \*   \*

Perhaps we may begin to rethink our reflexively negative reaction to violence by undemonizing the word itself, much as the Victorians had to learn not to rear up at the very mention of "sex." (Ironically, it was the Victorians who coined the modern, erotic sense of the word; before the mid-to-late-nineteenth century, "sex" mostly referred to gender.) The word "sex" was a thought-stopper to the Victorians, much as the word "violence" is to us, and we might try and push through that barrier by exploring the history of the word itself, which hums with complex and subtle echoes lost or faded in our current crude usage.

In previous centuries, *violence* and *violent* were more flexibly used to express a variety of vigorous actions, feelings or events that were not necessarily negative in intention. The Oxford English Dictionary provides shadings of *violent* or *violently* that were more commonly used in the past, such as "force or strength of physical action... vehemence of feeling... extreme ardor or fervor... strongly and impetuously... ardently, passionately." In Shakespeare's *King John*, a character describes his sense of urgency as being "scalded with my violent motion, and spleen of speed, to see your Majesty." [7] An early seventeenth-century travel book speaks of a rushing river that "carrieth so violent a streame that presently it is able to drive a mill." 8 In his 1697 *Aeneid*, Dryden speaks of "A love so violent, so strong, so sure,/ That neither age can change, nor art can cure." [9] Fifty or so years later Fielding says his hero Tom Jones concludes an assignation "by a fond caress, and many violent protestations of love," while Joseph Andrews, another Fielding hero, expresses his "violent respect" [10] for his lady. The current expression, to fall violently in love, echoes this old meaning, albeit with a hint of deliberate hyperbole.

These energetic senses of the word hark back to the presumed Indo-European root, *wi-*, and Medieval Latin *vis*, meaning *strength* or *vigor*. The Latin *violentia*, from which the English and other European words are directly derived, emphasized vehemence or impetuosity rather than attack, and the obsolete eighteenth century form of *violentness* was a synonym for sharpness, boisterousness and outrageousness.

Clearly, in those earlier times, when our tongue was being stretched and strengthened, the word violence had many more shadings than the one-dimensional sense popular today. Retrieving these old uses allows us to widen its meaning to include the sense of a forcefully charged emotion, atmosphere or event capable of enhancing experience across a broad spectrum of feeling and action.

It's clear, however, that violent energies operate at varying levels of crudity and refinement. At the basic level, they constitute a raw force with rough purposes for good as well as ill, erupting as the breaker of social, cultural and political deadlocks. Justified rebellions, righteous wars, evolutionary conquests, and all the varieties of revolt against oppression derive from this elemental impulse. This is the quality of violence Yeats called "a terrible beauty," a power disrupting the "casual comedy of everyday life." [11] We have to love even such bloody upheavals as warfare, Yeats declared in his essay, *On The Boiler*, because in their wake belief will be changed and civilization renewed.

This is the bluntest kind of violence. It is blunt in the manner in which it impacts people's lives and disrupts social stability, even if its overall effects are ultimately beneficial - but it may be, in Kafka's phrase, the only axe that can smash through a frozen sea. Blocked by a despotic government or a totally unresponsive regime, political action may have no alternative but an escalation of violence. For example, the Africans' armed and bloody insurrection in the 1970s against the Rhodesian government in the country of my birth was the only way to force the end of a morally indefensible minority rule in the nation that has become Zimbabwe. The fact that thirty thousand people had to die before the whites gave way was a measure of the Europeans' stubborn defense of privilege. Similarly, in South Africa, many thousands shed their blood before the racist government departed.

However, it is crucial that a clear sense of the apt response to the actual situation is maintained in all political interactions involving violence. What makes violence creative rather than destructive in these cases is always a consideration of the context, the conditions of any action, and the character of the participants; the actual complexion of these factors should always govern the forceful resolution of political and social tensions.

In a democracy, homosexuals, say, may only need to mount a verbally violent protest march to make the larger public aware that they have legitimate grievances requiring an equitable resolution. On the other hand, a class of socially neglected and economically deprived inner-city dwellers may have to riot and burn down their own neighborhoods to elicit action to ease their desperate plight. If homosexuals escalated their protest to the level of arson, or ghetto-dwellers upped the ante to armed revolt, the legitimacy of the violence involved might be fatally compromised. In politics, as in everyday life, the flow of action and reaction between one person and another, one group and another, depends always upon a lively and passionate awareness of what will enhance rather than diminish ourselves or others.

However, at the primal level of experience the violence involved may be appropriately extreme. This holds true in situations where any man or woman confronts the inherently terrifying reality of the human condition under the light of eternity. Oedipus puts out his eyes, Christ is crucified, Quixote attacks imaginary monsters with all the vigor of his lance, Ahab wrecks the Pequod and drowns, Kurtz answers horror with horror.

*   *   *

Let me emphasize at once that this book in no way glamorizes violence. Nor does it romanticize, glorify, or revel in it. On the other hand, neither does it demonize violence as some kind of basic affliction cursing our lives, an evil we can only helplessly suffer or deplore. Rather, it sets out to explore mankind's metamorphosis of violence into powerful facts and metaphors, pointing the way to a bold, subtle, dynamic understanding of our own natures, and the nature of life itself. I suggest that we might begin to recover these old wisdoms, opening our minds to the wide range of original acts and responses violence has powered and provoked over thousands of years at every level of human experience; initiatives that have had a tonic effect on our society, our culture, our spiritual life, and our arts.

All in all, our history reveals that violence has a special purpose for human beings; that, alone among all the earth's species, we can shape, maneuver and respond to violence with new forms of expression and existence; that we can ride the wild beast and make it leap and bound in marvelous and astonishing ways. In truth, our unique capacity for the transformation of violence can be celebrated as one of mankind's most profound contributions to life on earth.

# 1
# creative murder

*The man lies asleep, yet he's awake. He can't move his arms or legs, but he can hear his family and friends gathered together to mourn while the undertakers ready his coffin and the grave diggers make a hole in the ground to receive it. He's puzzled and terrified that people are ready to bury him while he's still alive, but he can't make a move to stop them.*

*Between the man in the casket and the world beyond is an impenetrable mist, a veil that cannot be penetrated. All he knows is that the people he loves most seem to be deliberately preparing to murder him.*

*The coffin is lowered into the ground, accompanied by the lamentations and prayers of the mourners. As the earth drums on the lid of his wooden box the man imagines he is howling and sobbing, but in fact he can't make a sound. The dreadful drumming continuous remorselessly, until his coffin is covered over, and terror tears at his heart.*

*Inside the wooden box the man lies buried, but intensely aware. His ears become accustomed to the minute noises of the subterranean world that is now* his eternal home. Somehow the air in his coffin stays fresh. The rhythm of his breathing is in harmony with the friction of the particles of earth rubbing one against the other beyond the wooden walls; it stays in tune with the scratchings of underground creatures moving through the soil, the slithering of earthworms, the stretching of the roots of trees and plants. Listening to these small sounds, as old as time, the man's panic eases, his heart stops pounding, he feels the deep delight of being at peace with all creation.

Suddenly, he hears another noise, terrible and potent, like an earthquake deep underground. As it comes inexorably closer he recognizes it as the bellowing of a bull - but what a bull! Its roaring sends shock waves through his casket.

Trapped in his timber tomb, the buried man shudders with fright. Is this oblivion come to claim him, extinguish his life forever? He has died and yet he lives. He has been through the realms of life and death, reconciled to both. Now total annihilation threatens his existence. The bellowing bull will blot him out, and that will be the end of memory, of being and becoming, of everything. As this feeling of terror escalates, however, it is answered by a rising fury, a terrible rage at nature's power to tear him apart, nullify his individual soul, make his life nothing. The fury is so hot it seems to set his heart aflame, warming his body from top to toe. For an eternal instant the heat of the interred man's rage matches the fires of hell.

Suddenly, the bull's head bumps his coffin with a frightful blow. The casket crumbles and the bull's skull crashes through the wood. The animal's hide is black as night and his eyes are yellow as the moon. The bull scoops the up body with his horns and carries him away, deeper into the earth, so deep the world is soundless, a depth beyond returning. The man's heart stops, his eyes flutter, he swoons. Everything goes black before his sight and he is *utterly wiped out.*

*When, after a seeming eternity, he regains con-
sciousness, he finds himself lying on the ground,
on the surface of the earth. It's a moonless night,
black as pitch, but he is alive. His soul soars with
ecstasy, with the joy of just being here. The thump-
ing of his heart, the feel of his bare skin on the damp
ground, the soft touch of the night air on his body
are an orgasm of being, a spasm of gladness in simply being alive.As he lies there, small as a newborn
baby cradled in the warm twigs and leaves, he feels
the wind of huge wings. A winged reindeer, white
as snow, flutters down upon him. She puts her teat
in his mouth and gives him suck. Her milk is inde-
scribably sweet, and so nourishing he grows back
to full manhood in a trice. And then, in the blink of
an eye, he is back on earth, in his old life, that is
completely new.*

\* \* \*

Spiritual journeys in many faiths often involve such annihilating yet exhilarating primal experiences. Some event of original sacred violence - an act of "creative murder," [12] in Mircea Eliade's
graphic phrase - is the fundamental organizing principle of almost
every religious structure mankind has contrived, from primitive worship to the theologies of contemporary churches. Few faiths or
mythologies lack a vital core of sacral violence, and almost all of the
major religions that dominate the world today, including Christianity, Islam and Judaism, honor some sort of violent event in the foundation of their beliefs. As Rudolf Otto observed, the experience of
the Holy follows a similar pattern in all cultures: *mysterium
tremendum, fascinans, augustum* (terror, rapture, majesty). [13]

Something has to die, and violently, before the soul's true life
can happen. "The heroic alpha-shaman goes out to meet the
predatorial danger, which takes him down to death to face the abys-
mal dragons of dismemberment," Rene Girard explained. "He returns reborn... with a tale to tell of how both the lust for killing and
the fear of dying may be transformed into energies that are life-
enhancing rather than life-denying." [14]

Spiritually ambitious souls willingly suffer the cruelest punishments, knowing that such suffering is the path to the sacred core of being. They walk on hot coals, pierce their bodies with knives, needles, nails and sharp sticks, blind themselves, starve themselves, cut out their own tongues, or sew the tips of the thumbs and forefingers of their left and right hands together to make a divine circle. A Siberian shaman told of being shot to death by the arrows of his ancestral spirits, who then cut him up, separated his bones, and ate his raw flesh before accepting him into their world.

Mystics and ecstatics of all traditions have courted such violent transformations with a lover's passion. Mechtild of Magdeburg, a thirteenth century German visionary, cried out to her god: "You are my mountain of glass, the feast of my eyes, the loss of my self, the storm of my heart, the dissolution and ruin of my nature, my highest security." [15] John Donne implored his Maker: "Batter my heart, three-person'd God... That I may rise, and stand, o'erthrow mee, and bend/ Your force, to breake, blowe, burn and make me new." [16]

"Pierce me with the arrows of your holy love!" [17] cried Armelle Nicolas, a seventeenth century French Catholic mystic. Fearing his heart would break in pieces, Nicolas ran madly from one room to another and threw himself on the floor, shrieking "Mercy, Lord, mercy!" Such violent ecstasies, derived from the Greek word, *ekstasis*, a "stepping out," draws gifted souls to suffer hideously painful raptures to seek a grace that catches fire. By means of such extremes Nicolas plunges into "the darkness of unknowing," into the embrace of divinity, beyond life and death. This is the condition the Oglalla Sioux call "Wakan-Tanka," The Great Mystery, the source of all wisdom, Mechtild's "highest security."

A medieval Islamic esoteric text that still inspires Muslim ecstatics exclaims: "Wrap yourself in the cloak of nothingness and drink from the cup of annihilation, cover your breast with the love of vanishing away, and set the burnoose of non-being on your head. When you have nothing more, think not even of a shroud, and throw yourself naked into the fire."[18] Annihilation is the Muslim Sufi's ticket to heaven. "God, you have made lawful my blood, kill me," [19] cried the mystic martyr Al-Hallaj, while being murdered by his religious enemies.

This extremity of being can only reached through ecstatic trance. "Ecstasy is originally an entering into God, *enthusiamos*, being filled with the god," [20] writes the Jewish metaphysician Martin Buber. The Hebrew sage Hai Gaon describes the moment the ecstatic enters into God after suffering the ten rungs of the mystical ascent. "Then heaven opens up before him...(and) something happens in his heart whereby he enters into the contemplation of things divine." [21] The medieval German mystic Meister Eckhart declared that the ecstatic, like the bride in the biblical Song of Songs, "reaches the dark power of the Father, where all speech ends." [22]

Acts of creative murder spark the creation of the world in the Sumerian-Akkadian creation epic, *Enuma Elish*, dating from the fourth millennium BC. The hero, Marduk, challenges Tiamat, the archetypal mother, to bloody battle. He attacks Tiamat with fierce winds which grossly inflate her stomach. "He then loosed an arrow, which perforated her belly, tore her entrails, and pierced her heart." [23] After chaining Tiamat's firstborn son, Kingu, Marduk turns on Tiamat and splits her skull and body in two; one half became the sky, the other the earth. Later, Kingu is also sacrificed; his veins are cut and mankind is made from his blood.

Similarly, in the Egyptian cosmogony, the primal god Osiris is dismembered by his brother, Set. Osiris' son Horus is sodomized by Set and blinded in one eye. In terror he fears the Land of the Dead might be carved from his violated bowels, but he manages to subdue his rampant uncle. Later, Osiris' wife Isis is beheaded by her blinded son; but she survives to give him back his sight, which Horus offers to his father, restoring him to life. Osiris becomes King of the Underworld, bestowing immortality upon all his worshippers.

Forms of cosmic violence predate even these ancient stories. An early seventh millennium BC mural found at Catal Huyuk, in Western Anatolia, shows a vulture, an avatar of the Great Goddess, swooping down on headless corpses. The vulture is "She Who Takes Away Life, maleficent twin of She Who Gives Life," [24]. The fact that the vultures are painted in red, the color of life, rather than black signifies the Goddess's power of regeneration. The Vulture Goddess snatches the soul, only to restore it to life in another form. Pain and death are part of life in the Great Goddess's realm, and annihilation breeds renewal.

In yet other versions of creative murder, angry or disgusted divine fathers destroy their own creations, as Jehovah does in the great flood, to give the world a fresh start. Noah and his few Ark companions survive to begin mankind's adventure again. Many centuries after the Flood, the prophet Daniel had a vision in which four dangerous beasts - a lion, a bear, a leopard, and a fourth creature with ten horns and iron teeth - emerged from the sea while the Ancient of Days, sitting upon a throne of fire, predicted the devastation of kingdoms.

Creative killing describes the brutal battle between Uranus and his son Cronos in the Hellenic creation myth. Cronos castrates his father with a sickle and Uranus' blood gives birth to the Erinyes, the terrible goddesses of vengeance. Yet Aphrodite, goddess of love, is also born from this brutal act; Uranus's sexual organs fall into the sea and his sperm, *aphros*, inseminates the frothy waves.

The Greek semi-deity, Dionysus, was the archetype of the sacrificial king later embodied by Christ: the god-like man whose violent death generates new possibilities. According to one version of the Dionysus passion, the demigod was torn to shreds on the orders of Zeus's wife, Hera. The man-god's dismembered limbs were boiled in a cauldron by the Titans, then eaten; but a pomegranate tree sprouted from the soil where his blood was spilled, and he was reborn. A similar fate awaited the splendidly handsome Adonis, lover of the rival goddesses Persephone and Aphrodite - darkness and light, winter and summer. Gored to death by the war god Ares in the guise of a wild boar, Adonis's blood still germinates the host of red anemones that each spring carpet rocky Greek hillsides.

For the Hellenes, the unique gift of consciousness itself was born in violence. For giving mankind the gift of fire, stolen from heaven, Prometheus was punished by Zeus, who sent an eagle to eat his liver. The gods feared that the gift of fire - sentience - would allow men to challenge their power. Caught between opposing forces of nature and consciousness, human beings faced a world that "ever was, and is, and shall be, ever-living Fire, in measures being kindled and in measures going out," [25] Heraclitus declared. But without the energies of such conflict nothing vibrant would be created, for every opportunity for harmony and love comes out of turbulence, "since the mixture which is not shaken decomposes."

Elements of Prometheus and Dionysus are fused in the North American "trickster" figure, called Coyote. Coyote steals flames from the Fire People by deliberately catching their blaze in his headdress. Like Prometheus, he is a criminal. However, he not only steals fire, he also lies, cheats and seduces innocent women. He is an anarchist, creating chaos and disorder wherever he goes.

In one hilariously unpleasant episode he defecates so mightily he buries the earth itself in a skyscraper of shit. Coyote, seated on the peak of this odorous tower, slips and falls, and ends up blinded by his own excreta. But Coyote, like the wild Greek demigod Dionysus, is the father of all human culture. His shit is fertile, and the fire he brings to men inflames their hearts and minds. [26]

In the Buddhist metaphysic, the human soul, suspended between the impure kingdom of worldly transmigration, *samsara*, and the pure rapture of the great void, *nirvana*, works through its personal fate. But unlike the combative Greeks, Buddhists surrender to their fate. Where *samsara* and *nirvana* are fused all opposites and dualities are dissolved. However, a violent metaphor is used to describe the ultimate spiritual state of grace in which the yogic devotee "annihilates" the cycle of existence.

Hinduism contributes its vision of worldly illusion or samsara as a dream or nightmare of Vishnu, the Creator. Vishnu is accompanied by Shiva, god of fire and a wild hunter, the Destroyer of the Universe. The image of Shiva dancing depicts destructive and creative powers in a dynamic process of perpetual disintegration and renewal. Shiva lives in a ring of fire. He holds a tongue of flame in his left hand and a drum signifying ethereal sound in his right, while crushing the demon of worldly illusion underfoot. In this image the ferocity of natural forces is seen harnessed against itself, conjuring up a spiritual world in which man may create his own soul.

The Vedic goddess Kali, the Indian World Mother, is a complex figure symbolizing, like Shiva, both creation and destruction. With her necklace of skulls, Kali represents violence and death; but her breath, in Hindu mystic Sri Ramakrishna's view, "gives out the soothing touch of tender love and the seed of immortality." For Ramakrishna, Kali "appears to be reeling under the spell of wine - but who would create this mad world unless under the influence of divine drunkenness?" [27] Indra, the *Rig Veda's* most popular god, establishes his authority by slaying the dragon Vrtra with a thunderbolt, then splitting its head, freeing the waters of life.

An act of metaphysical violence enlivens the core of the mystical cosmogony of Isaac Luria, the great sixteenth century Hebrew

Kabbalist. In Luria's vision, the vessels receiving the original divine emanations are drastically shattered, scattering divine sparks from the fire of "judgment" into the mud of the world's impurity. This primal "breaking of the vessels" begins mankind's spiritual task, the struggle to restore the fallen sparks to their divine realm. The original shattering has given human beings the chance to share in recreating the universal unity; without that radical disruption, they would have no spiritual purpose.

*   *   *

Apart from the mythologies of creative murder, some act of symbolic or actual sacrificial killing often lies at the heart of humanity's original apprehension of the sacred. "*Homo religiosus* acts and attains self-awarenes as *homo necans*," (killer) [28] Walter Burkert suggested. "[Social] solidarity was achieved through a sacred crime with due reparation." [29] Sacred crimes such as these engender a cultural cohesion, a sense of original, collective salvation. "You saved us by shedding blood," the devotees of Mithra praised their bull-slaying god. "What has become a mystic paradox had been just a fact in the beginning." [30]

It does not matter that such primal "facts" become obscured as a religion or a culture evolves. As Rene Girard remarked, "We can identify the commemoration in mythology of these same violent acts that are so successful [in their collective repercussions] that they force their perpetrators to reenact them. This memory inevitably develops as it is transmitted from generation to generation..." [31] It may be, as Girard continues, that "instead of rediscovering the secret of its original distortion it loses it over and over again, each time burying it a little deeper. As religion and cultures are formed and perpetuated, the violence is hidden."

Whether buried fact or mystic paradox, the original violence powering the sacred continues to energize almost every variety of faith. Violence is the "heart and secret soul" [32] of the sacred, Girard said, and it has long been a profoundly human act to ritualize our vital savageries.

Acts of sacral violence occur in almost every agrarian culture. Among the Ibibio people of southern Nigeria, for instance, the supreme female creator Eka Abassi gives birth to her son, Obumo, who is also her husband. At the annual festival of the New Yams, chosen lepers are wrapped in palm bark and tied to a tree trunk. The victim, his face eaten away by the horrible disease, is bound to the palm by the waist and throat and arms, as if he were making love to the yam tree. His feet are pinned to the ground with hooked pegs, and he dies, crucified, in a long, slow agony under the sun. [33]

The link between bloody sacrifice and religious affirmation is one of the meanings of Abraham's acceptance of Jehovah's command to plunge a knife into his beloved son Isaac's chest. Although the Bible says that God ordered Isaac's death as a burnt offering to test Abraham's faith, the fact that the patriarch accepted the order without protest reveals his profound acceptance of the connection between violent sacrifice and a sacred covenant. This symbolic act, interrupted by an angel, brought a divine promise that Abraham's seed would multiply as "the stars of heaven." [34]

The image of Isaac on the funeral pyre is echoed in the Christian Crucifixion. Indeed, Jesus's savage death on the cross is one of history's most powerful symbols of creative sacrifice. Spat upon, beaten and mocked by Roman soldiers, crowned with thorns and nailed to the cross on Golgotha; bleeding, dying slowly, crying out that he was forsaken, Jesus has to suffer torments and death to sear his spiritual message into the hearts of generations to come. The Crucifixion's brutal, iconic imagery reminds us that the redemptive love Christ offers his devotees is tempered by an absolute agony.

In the *Revelation of St. John the Divine*, lighting and thunder pour from the heavenly throne, which is guarded by four beasts and lit by the fire of the seven lamps of God. God's book, sealed with seven seals, is closed to human eyes, until Jesus, God's pure Lamb, comes along. "Worthy is the Lamb that was slain to receive power, and riches, and wisdom, and strength, and honor, and glory, and blessing." [35] Spilt blood is Christianity's central symbol. It is Christ's seed, said Tertullian, a second century Christian. "We multiply whenever we are mown down by you," [36] he declared, challenging the vicious Roman persecution of the young sect. Martyrs create faith, faith does not create martyrs, remarked the nineteenth-century Spanish philosopher Miguel de Unamuno. Those who died violently set the tone for Christianity's conquest of millions of souls.

If he had not been crucified, Christ's message would likely have been lost among the preachings of the host of self-proclaimed prophets populating Palestine in his time. As it is, Christianity's central symbol became a metaphor of transcendence; a metaphor that does not deny the essential role of the violence that gives it its primal potency. At the same time, the Crucifixion celebrates the unique human capacity to transmute such brute reality through the power of man's spirit and imagination.

Over the centuries, the image of the Crucifixion has opened a deep well of feeling in the human heart. Christ died at the hands of the humanity he came to save, and the Crucifixion is a supreme symbol of a man fruitfully sacrificed to his own spirituality. The figure of the wounded saviour hanging on the cross symbolizes a holy marriage, a fertile *hieros gamos* of those dynamic polarities the Presocratic philosopher Empedocles characterized as Love and Strife.

Love and Strife are the twin powers that rule the world, Empedocles declared. Love is the force that seeks cohesion, while Strife is the energy that disrupts, allowing new possibilities to be born. "I shall tell thee a two-fold tale. There is a double becoming of perishable things and a double passing away. The coming together of all things brings one generation into being and destroys it." [37] In Empedocles's view, "The blood around men's hearts is their thinking." [38] Echoing Empedocles, Immanuel Kant observed that, while human beings might imagine they desire harmony, nature wills discord, so that "man may be impelled to a new exertion of his powers, and to the further development of his natural capacities." [39].

Despite its central importance, the act of creative murder epitomized in the Crucifixion took centuries to achieve its crucial role in the Christian imagination. Indeed, the Crucifixion did not become Christianity's dominant icon until the ninth century, in the reign of the Emperor Charlemagne. Earlier images of Jesus rendered him most frequently as an infant in his mother's arms or as a shepherd among woolly lambs. They presented him as a teacher, or as the Byzantine Pantocrator: the dark, scowling, almost demonic visage staring down at human folly from the rim of heaven. But when Christianity began to assume its primacy in Western Europe's life, the Crucifixion became its core symbol.

The earlier representations of the Crucifixion itself were crude, inspired by the blunt notion of agony itself as redemption rather than a weapon in the struggle for salvation. "The more the flesh is wasted by affliction, so much the more is the spirit strengthened by inward grace," [40] declared the *Imitato Christi*, a highly popular fifteenth century manuscript attributed to Thomas à Kempis. Taking him literally, fanatical believers committed acts of ferocious self-injury, gnawing off their own hands, scratching their faces to a bloody pulp, tearing out clumps of their own hair in pursuit of divine grace.

It took the talents of artists to elevate such literal barbarities into visual metaphors illuminating the true significance of the Crucifixion. Painters and sculptors, from the anonymous tenth century carver of the Cross of Gero in Cologne Cathedral to Matthias Grunewald, poured their talents into rendering the Crucifixion's inherent profundity.

In his 1515 altarpiece for the chapel in the Alsatian monastery of St. Anthony of Isenheim, Grunewald portrayed the raw agony of the tortured man nailed to the cross - yet calmly contemplated by a woolly lamb, representing a flock of worshippers. In its wise innocence, the lamb understands why his master has to be crucified to validate his claim to be a real savior.

Grunewald's altarpiece presents one of the most searing Crucifixions ever painted. It portrays a Christ whose flesh is torn and bruised as if dragged through a razor-wire fence. His head is slumped, his mouth agape, his brow bloodied by a crown of thorns. His fingers gesticulate in agony above the nailed palms. This is a man tormented from within, and Grunewald mercilessly puts damnation where it belongs, not in some external circumstance or cruel ignorance but inside the envelope of each man's soul. Grunewald's Jesus is an individual of the kind celebrated by Renaissance humanists: a particular, suffering person, the artist of his own despair, the victim of his own doubt. This is the Redeemer who cries, "Lord, Lord, why hast thou forsaken me?"

The power of the Crucifixion as a primal image of sacred sacrifice is still very much alive. However, in the versions of twentieth century artists, such as the Mexican painter Frida Kahlo and the Englishman Francis Bacon, the symbolism has become completely personal, totally internalized. The crucified subject in their paintings is not Jesus but themselves, and the act of art itself, not the religious transcendence of a Grunewald Crucifixion, is their private transformation.

Kahlo's striking 1944 canvas, *The Broken Column*, painted after she had undergone surgery for a terrible accident that injured her spine, depicts the painter bare to the waist, her breast slashed in two by a crumbling classical column. Nails of pain pierce her flesh

**11**

in this female Crucifixion, and only the bonds of a crude orthopedic corset keep the tortured body from flying apart. "To hope with anguish retained," [41] Kahlo wrote in her diary about this work.

Bacon's crucifixions present gritty, ectoplasmic icons of pyschosexual atrocity. In his canon, these images are joined by silently screaming Popes, demented, paranoid portraits, obscenely compelling studies of the human body, and carcasses slung from butcher hooks. All these are rendered in moods that recall Michelangelo's flayed St Bartholomew in his *Last Judgment* fresco in the Sistine Chapel. In Michelangelo's vision, the flayed skin of the martyred saint hangs like a loose cloth on a hook; the stripped face - the artist's own - is a slurred and horrible mask drooping in the middle of the chest.

Bacon's art teeters on the edge of a pornography of violence, but its saving grace springs from a tonic energy. In his view, salaciousness is in the eye of the man who watches rather than the man who paints. The viewer, who is the artist himself as well as the museum or gallery visitor who looks into Bacon's world, shares a potent attraction-revulsion that can excite or poison him. Still, even in this state of fright, the shadow of a violence-bred transcendence lingers on.

Transcendence born of violence also charges the theology of Islam. One Muslim tradition has it that Muhammad, God's Apostle, was thrown down to earth from heaven by two angels, who tore open his chest, snatched a drop of black blood, and washed his entrails with melting snow. [42]

The martyrdom of the Imam Husseini, a direct descendant of Muhammad, is the central Passion of the powerful Shi'ite sect that dominates today's Iran. Defeated at the battle of Karbala, Iraq, in 680 AD by leaders of the rival Sunnis, Husseini was brutally stoned to death and beheaded. Shi'ias reenact this gory event in the annual Muharram rites, down to the display, before grieving multitudes, of a replica of the severed Imam's bleeding head. Every year a few zealots goad themselves into a frenzy of self-mutilation in this Imitatio Husseini, spilling their blood in the dust, reaffirming the potency of the original creative murder that powers their faith.

However, the most brutally honest and elaborately orchestrated acts of religious murder occurred in the Mayan-Aztec rituals. In those terrifying yet joyously magnificent blood ceremonies, chosen men, women and children were sacrificed as demigods and victims rolled into one.

At the beginning of autumn, in their capital Tenochtitlan, the Aztecs celebrated the harvest festival of Ochpaniztli. "The first eight days of Ochpanitzli they danced without singing and without playing the teponaztli," the Spanish monk, Fray Bernardino de Sahagun, recorded. "After these eight days the woman representing the image of Teteuinna appeared dressed in the ornaments of that image." [43] She was the chosen sacrificial *ixiptla*, or god-impersonator.

In the first week of the Ochpaniztli festival, men and women switched roles. Warriors marched through the streets carrying flowering branches in their hands, while women staged mock military skirmishes in the temple precincts. At the peak of the ceremony the dazed, drugged *ixiptla* moved through the central marketplace accompanied by dancers and flute players, scattering seeds as she went. That night she was hurried to the pyramid of the corn god. Spreadeagled upon the back of a kneeling priest, her face turned toward the stars, she was decapitated. Her torso was flayed by a naked priest, who slipped into her wet skin and descended the pyramid to greet the crowd of warriors waiting there.

The "sacred crime" played out in this ritual is so potent and so direct its mere recital numbs our minds. Yet it reveals an extraordinary spiritual courage. The often hideously cruel gods of the sky, the capricious sun and the moon whose rhythms controlled the earth's fertility were boldly confronted. Like Christ's crucifixion, the Aztec human sacrifice was a symbolic act rendered in the flesh. In both cases a god-impersonator dies so that mankind might live, and such collective acts of creative murder provide the paradox of hope for an eternal life.

# 2
# killing eternity

Imagine a rich and influential man, respected, even revered for the good he's done to others. He's at the height of his prosperity and power, his family and friends love him. His life has gone well, blessed by good fortune, and all his ambitions seem fulfilled. He appears to have entered, in his prime, into a period of peace, a feeling of profound conjunction between his personal fate, the flow of the period in which he lives, and the commandments of the god he worships.

This is a proud man, but one who has much to be proud about. In fact, he counts his pride as the driving force that has pushed him to seek power with honor. Power tempered by honor, honor tempered by power, are crucial to his intuitive sense of that universal balance of forces which he fancies is the reflection of a divine order.

In the quiet moments he enjoys in the midst of a busy and fulfilling life, he may dare to think of himself as blessed. Somehow everything has worked out for him. Perhaps he reproaches himself for some confused and doubtful things he's done, mostly when he was young and inexperienced, and hot to make his mark. But he shuns the self-indulgence of guilt. Not that he has nothing to blame himself for; but to whip up these old, minor shames into a froth would be sentimental, a vulgar feeling in excess of the facts, a distortion of his proper sense of how a man should behave.

In truth, our man feels thoroughly in tune with fate. However, he knows he must be constantly alert and not sink into a complacency induced by his good fortune. Alertness is essential to maintain the vital circle of existence, and in being alert, he feels secure against radical surprise.

But then, for reasons he can't fathom, things go wrong. Suddenly, this happy and successful man is knocked off his pedestal of power and prosperity. For no seeming fault of his own, he faces catastrophe and humiliation at the hands of a capricious Fate - a Fate he imagined he understood and honored. Life is terribly out of whack, and all the old laws of existence appear to have been trashed in a frenzy of wild injustice.

It's a terrible moment. The proud man's mental and emotional house, that he's worked so long and hard to build, is a ruin. The mortar that binds the bricks of his spirit crumbles away, the protective walls come tumbling down. His ears are filled with the sound of their crashing, and the dust blinds his eyes. There seems no way to account for the cruelty of this destruction of everything he's striven for all his life. In the depths of his despair he agonizes over his response to a brutal fate.

This is the trial Job faces in the Bible. Ruined by a Deity who cannot resist a wager with Satan to test the limits of an exemplary man's faith, Job endures the loss of his animals, the murder of his servants, a devastating fire, the death of his sons and daughters, and a plague of painful boils. Everyone says he must have done something horrible to be so afflicted. "Whoever perished, being innocent?" asks one of the three friends who come to counsel him in his distress. Why does Job still hold fast to his integrity, his wife demands, urging him to curse God and die.

But dying would be a surrender. When an imperious Deity demands: "Have you an arm like God? And can you thunder with a voice like Him?" - Job boldly retorts: "I will demand of thee, and declare thou unto me." Instead of collapsing in submission, Job tears his clothes, shaves his head and covers himself in dust and ashes. "Let the day perish wherein I was born," he cries, profaning his life and, by inference, God's purpose in creating him; "let the blackness of the day terrify it." [44]

Adding rebellion to the sin of revulsion at his own birth, Job cries out: "What is man, that thou shouldest magnify him? And that thou shouldest set thine heart upon him? And that thou shouldest visit him every morning, and try him every moment?" [45]

You made me, and now you want to destroy me, he says; but I will go down fighting, contending, answering ferocious suffering with furious questions. Job's final repentance, in dust and ashes, for the sin of being human, is perfunctory. His victory lies in having opposed Jehovah's violence with a powerful counter-violence generated by his own spirit.

The essence of Job's challenge to heaven lies in this key question: Should a man just lie down and take the terrible blows destiny has laid upon him? Should he accept his sufferings as a lesson in humility at the hands of the gods, racking his brains to discover how he might have provoked his punishments by somehow betraying the natural order? Or should he, like Job, face up to fate with the higher pride that marks him as a human being?

*　*　*

As the civilizations of the eastern Mediterranean matured in the millennium before the birth of Christ, two major literary modes evolved out of the fertile mix of cultures: the dramatic art the Greeks called tragedy, and the tragical-allegoric form epitomized by the *Book of Job*. (The crucial section of the *Book of Job* known as The Dialogue dates from the seventh century BC, according to recent biblical scholarship, while Sophocles wrote *Oedipus Rex* around 430 BC.)

The authors of these new tragedies and radical allegories took a huge step forward in the history of human consciousness. They dared challenge the very basis of the human condition under an alternately demanding and indifferent heaven, directly confronting the violence of creation with a creative violence of their own. Together, these new literary genres added a powerful new weapon in man's long struggle to grasp the significance of his place on earth, in a situation that seemed to single him out among all the other creatures on the planet, while doing its best to crush his unique spirit.

Miguel de Unamuno captured the basic intention of the tragic mode in his comment that, while killing time is the essence of comedy, the essence of tragedy is killing eternity. [46] Eternity - in the sense of an extra-human dimension without beginning or end, free of concern for anyone's fate - is the fundamental threat to any sense of purpose in the life of Unamuno's man of flesh and blood, "the one who is born, suffers and dies - above all, who dies." [47] What Unamuno called the tragic sense of life has to do with our necessity to attack the abstract dimension that discounts our personal agonies and mocks our individual and collective mortalities.

Tragedy is the account of the contest in which mankind combats the eternal reality that vitiates humanity's best ecstasies and worst sufferings. What makes mankind's situation tragic, Joseph Conrad said, is not that we are victims of nature, but that we are conscious of our victimhood. "As soon as you know of your slavery, the pain, the anger, the strife - the tragedy begins." [48] D.H. Lawrence declared that "Tragedy ought really to be a great kick at misery." [49]

A great kick at misery describes King Oedipus's action in putting out his eyes with Jocasta's golden brooches, when he discovers his mother/wife has hanged herself in shame. As the blood bursts from his sockets, Oedipus, unwittingly incestuous, curses the horrors of his own doing and invents a violent darkness to match the dark violence of the gods.

In mutilating himself, Oedipus becomes his own man, answering divine judgment with a very human anguish, asserting his unique individuality in the face of the cruel twists of fate. Though it is Apollo who has laid this agony upon him, he has chosen his own punishment, a torment far more graphic than the god contrived. The Chorus may claim that the demons of destiny have ridden him down, but Oedipus struggles to hold his ground, answering divine terror with a self-willed, violent suffering. "*I* did it!" he declares. "The blinding hand was my own."

Shelley, following Aristotle's famous definition of dramatic catharsis, wrote that in the Athenian tragedies, "The imagination is enlarged by a sympathy with pains and passions so mighty, that they distend in their conception the capacity of that by which they are conceived; the good affections are strengthened by pity, indignation, terror and sorrow; and an exalted calm is prolonged from the satiety of this high exercise of them into the tumult of familiar life." [50]

However, the ultimate power of tragedy reaches beyond any catharsis of pity, indignation, terror and sorrow. Merely suffering the depredations of the demons of destiny, no matter how pitifully or terribly, does not engender a truly tragic drama. The quality of tragedy that most strengthens the human spirit and imagination depends upon the hero's capacity to answer the violence of creation with a violent creativity of his own.

The tragic vision, Nietzsche said, "sees man as a questioner, naked, unaccommodated, alone, facing mysterious demonic forces in his own nature and outside, and the irreducible facts of suffering and death." [51] In order to live at all, the Hellenes had to "triumph over a dreadful insight into the depths of reality and an intense susceptibility to suffering [by means of] powerful and joyful illusions." [52] To kill eternity, a tragic hero must conjure up those powerful and joyful illusions, and the bold ferocity of his own despair. At the same time, he seldom seems surprised by the inevitability of suffering. "Why do you weep for the death of your son, when it avails you nothing?" a skeptic asked Solon, the great Athenian lawgiver. "I weep precisely because it avails nothing," Solon replied.

In the sense we have been discussing, the *Iliad* is less profoundly tragical than *Oedipus Rex* or *The Book of Job*. None of Homer's heroes challenge the violence of the gods in the radical way that distinguishes Oedipus or Job. In the Iliad, the gods simply choose up sides between the Achaians and the Trojans, and there is none of the clear opposition between the Olympian and the human realm found in the true tragic form of *Oedipus Rex* or *The Book of Job*, where the supernatural and the human exist on distinctly separate planes.

Homer's gods and demons, though still terrible and potent, are above, below and outside the earth on which men live. It is the clear division of the human and the extra-human that allows Oedipus to challenge Apollo in a manner inconceivable even to a warrior as bold and fierce as Achilles. It took the radical, eternity-killing stance of the true tragic hero to show that this turbulent, dangerous, god-ridden world could only be confronted in a truly human fashion if men found the courage and imagination to conjure up their own creative violence.

Sophocles's Oedipus, and the Job created by unknown poets, are essentially innocent victims of a divine realm that capriciously singles them out for agony. The integrity of their innocence, coupled with a vehement retort to the heavens, is the original tragic hero at his purest. The hero may be shaken to his roots by the actions of a terrible fate; but, after the initial shock, he generates his own forceful response.

Job's reaction to Jehovah springs from the same kind of defiant humility that moved Oedipus in his confrontation with Apollo. Both Oedipus the proud king and Job the prosperous landowner try the boundaries of their humanity by contesting the extra-human realities that surround them. Under extremity, they extend the meaning of their lives while stretching the outer limits of mankind's moral and spiritual territories. Emerging from the mists of an old subservience to heaven and hell, Oedipus and Job, those twin tragic icons, present a crucial evolution in humanity's perception of its place in the cosmos.

Oedipus and Job are pillars of the great traditions, Hellenic and Hebraic, which constitute the structure of the Western mind. Oedipus's cry, "*I* did it!" is the proudest claim of Western civilization, ringing down the ages to our own day.

*       *       *

After the Golden Age of Athens in the fifth century BC, true tragic drama, in the sense of a hero answering the violence of creation with a powerful creative violence of his own, seemed to disappear for almost two thousand years. The plays, poems and other literary works that fall between *Oedipus Rex* and Dante's *Divine Comedy* often revert to an earlier mode in which the human, the natural and the supernatural worlds are intermingled. They deal with heroic struggles to endure rather than confrontations with an eternity that must be challenged, or even killed.

The reasons for this long hiatus remain mysterious only if one imagines that the evolution of human consciousness is strictly linear. Men of the dimension to test the calibre of the species are rare, and they must emerge from a context of confidence, from a culture that believes its highest spirits can ride out the demons of destiny.

When the tragic drama did reemerge in Renaissance Florence in the early fourteenth century, it added an extra dimension: it offered heroes who more or less chose to test the high courage of their hearts, rather than wait to have an Apollo or a Jehovah seek them out. Where Oedipus and Job were undeservedly struck down by external and capricious deities, the new tragic hero decides - deliberately, or driven by some powerful inner necessity - to test the boundaries of his humanity by initiating a journey into the depths of his own soul.

The soul, in the sense that Renaissance poets and dramatists such as Dante, Marlowe and Shakespeare conceived it, was a Christian invention. It suggests an inwardness neither Oedipus or Job would have fully grasped; a quality beyond time and space, which is simultaneously immortal and the personal ground of the battle waged in every human breast. For the Greeks or Hebrews, this kind of intense inwardness had no real language. They felt no need for such constant self-questioning. With Christianity, however, the demons of destiny set up house inside the personal psyche. Both the sky above and the earth below become the context rather than the core of man's struggle to be fully human.

These new tragedies implicitly recognized that the eternal dimension that had plagued Oedipus and Job was not some cosmic abstraction so much as a uniquely human perception; a concept born out of the primal terror lurking in our hearts, the sense of an ultimate insignificance mocking all our agonies. Eternity, in other words, was folded into the fabric of the human spirit.

In this more modern dramatic form the action takes place on a completely human plane. Gods and devils, insofar as they are called up, are mostly metaphors for the forces within men's breasts. In a war of man with himself, the hero risks everything, and in the fight comes close to discovering the essence of his existence. As Bataille put it: "To go to the end of man, it is necessary, at a certain point, to no longer submit, but to force one's destiny." [53]

Dante's literary alter ego finds himself astray in a darkling wood. He claims he doesn't quite grasp how he got there, but he knows it is where he has to be, in a place "whose memory renews the first dismay." [54] He is bitter, but he recognizes that his life has inevitably led him to this pass.

The poet deliberately descends into an imagined world, an inferno of the dead, with the poet Virgil as his guide. He trembles for fear of madness, encounters the Lady Beatrice, and his dark journey is lit by a ray of divine light - an illumination sharpened by terror. "Less than a drop of blood remains in me that does not tremble; I recognize the signals of the ancient flame." [55]

Dante suffered his own version of what medieval theology called *felix culpa*, the fortunate fault or fall, in which a sinner's struggle generates his spiritual rebirth. St. Augustine ascribed the original *felix culpa* to Adam and Eve who, in his view, created the necessity of the eventual coming of the Redeemer by their fall from grace.

Dante's descent, however, was crucially different from Adam and Eve's; unlike the Bible's first couple, whose real sin was innocence, a knowingly corrupted Dante intentionally chose to enter the place whose memory renewed the first dismay.

In Dante, the urge for a regeneration of the spirit was tempered by an essentially Hellenic delight in the freedom of the human will, "with which the creatures with intelligence, they all and they alone, were and are endowed." [56] The tragic vision of *The Divine Comedy* fuses the humanist morality of the Hellenes with the spiritual ethics of the Hebrews, and Dante's anguish derives from Job's basic query: What is man?

In the Florentine poet's sensibility this question is elaborated by the Christian doctrine of original sin, and by that sense of living out a descent into creation from the plane of the divine described by Plotinus, the third century Alexandrian Greek Neoplatonist. But the foundations of Dante's brave spirit were strengthened by the old Greek faith in the garment of the mind, a belief in man as the measure of all things. Where Job's Jehovah and Oedipus's Apollo were godly presences, Dante's Virgil was an historic human figure, Beatrice a real woman, and Dante's Inferno, Purgatory and Paradise were essentially the territories of his own self-awareness.

Around three hundred years after Dante composed his epic poem, two Englishmen imagined journeys of their own into the darkling wood of the human condition. Like Dante, Christopher Marlowe and William Shakespeare projected heroes who consciously or out of inner necessity chose to confront the terrors of eternity.

In *Doctor Faustus*, the first major Elizabethan tragedy, written in 1588, Marlowe's hero offers his soul to an imagined Lucifer - his other, darker self - in exchange for twenty-four years of the realization of everything he desires. As Mephistopheles points out, the God Faustus serves is his own violent desire for knowledge. Faustus believes that man is human because he is impelled by the passion to know the world, and himself: "This night I'll conjure though I die therefore." At the climax of the drama he cries out: "Stand still, you ever-moving spheres of heaven,/That time may cease and midnight never come." [57] In a weak final moment, Faustus calls to Lucifer that he will burn his books, but this last frailty does not diminish the boldness of his original endeavor. "He goes out no sinner but violently, speaking the rage and despair of all mankind who would

**21**

undo the past and stop the clock against the inevitable reckoning." [58]

Like Marlowe's Faustus, Shakespeare's King Lear is impelled to test the limits of his spirit. But while Faustus makes a knowing bargain with Lucifer, Lear is driven by an inner necessity that seems to take him by surprise.

Moved by some vague darker purpose, Lear divides his kingdom between two of his daughters, and willfully misunderstands the motives of Cordelia, his youngest and most loving child. Lear's stated reasons for this drastic change in his life fail to explain his astonishing actions. He's old, he says, and wishes to shake off worldly things while crawling toward his death. But in truth he's driven by an unconscious urge to challenge the approach of an eternity that must be killed before it kills him. By his strange, almost cavalier divestment of authority, Lear initiates a journey into the heart of darkness ruled by the original horror of the human condition.

The darkness captures him swiftly. In short order Lear is betrayed by Goneril and Regan, whom he dubs tigers, not daughters. He mourns the deliberate blinding of the Earl of Gloucester. Machinations, hollowness, treachery and all ruinous disorders follow men to their graves, Gloucester laments, and Lear learns the truth of this all too well.

The disenfranchised monarch encounters the full fury of raw nature, human and elemental. Men are capable of terrible ferocities, and Lear goes mad in the midst of a fierce storm. Demented, Lear wanders the wild heath, shouting his dare at heaven. "Blow winds, and crack your cheeks! Rage, blow! ... You sulfurous and thought-executing fires,/Vaunt-couriers of oak-cleaving thunderbolts,/Singe my white head!" [59] When Kent warns him that human nature can't carry such afflictions, Lear retorts: "Let the great gods,/That keep this dreadful pother o'er our heads,/Find out their enemies now." [60]

Lear deepens and refines his spirit in the fury of the suffering he has brought down upon his own head. Through the sheer frenzy of his madness he reinvents himself as a human being in the light of a murderous eternity. In this act of reinvention, Lear's original self-pity becomes a generous sympathy for others. Witnessing a whore being publicly lashed, Lear suffers with the woman. Lamenting the hanging of his poor Fool, Lear plumbs the depths of an agonized compassion. At the end of the play, Lear, carrying the dead

Cordelia in his arms, feels his heart split with the fury of his grief.

One of the underlying themes of *King Lear* is man's changing relationship with nature. The storm on the heath is wild and fierce, yet Lear is no mute and passive victim. He calls upon the cataracts and hurricanoes to do their worst, to spout until they've drenched the steeples; he exhorts the thunder to crack the mold that made mankind. And the storm, while retaining its own primal ferocity, mirrors the intensity in Lear's own breast. What this signifies is that Nature has become largely emblematic in the Age of Humanism; the new tragic hero fights his demons on a battlefield in which agitated nature is a dramatic reflection of his personal war. In this conflict man confronts his most terrifying adversary - himself. He faces head-on the wild beast of human nature for which, as Plato said, no crime is inconceivable.

Cervantes' Don Quixote is another Renaissance hero whose madness is a means to try the quality of his soul. In a burst of inspired craziness, the aging Knight of the Doleful Countenance conjures up the trappings of a vanished world of chivalry few sensible minds took seriously in the early seventeenth century. The Don is an old buffoon who becomes a hero through the extremity of his buffoonery. He begins as a toothless, wispy-locked, would-be knight errant in old and moldy armor with a barber's brass basin for a helmet. Riding his rawboned nag Rosinante, accompanied by his cowardly, mocking squire, Sancho Panza, he imagines damsels in distress crying out for rescue from mythical monsters.

Quixote's undeniable feats of courage may be figments of wild fantasy, but they are true measures of his soul's dimension nonetheless; in the caldron of his fervent fancy, Quixote cooks up the terrors he needs to feel truly human and alive. He carries his banner with pride even as he endures terrible pain. The windmills, that Quixote decides are a host of monstrous giants, send Rosinante and her rider rolling across the plain with such rough force the knight is stunned. An enraged muleteer punches him so hard his mouth is filled with blood. Yet in his high heart the battered old Don is happy, knowing that his hard struggle is his glorious hope. "The tragic artist is not a pessimist," Nietzsche pointed out. "He says `Yes' to everything terrible and problematical." [61] Vladimir Nabokov, who called *Don Quixote* one of the most bitter and barbarous books ever

penned, concluded: "We do not laugh at him any longer. His bla-
zon is pity, his banner is beauty. He stands for everything that is
gentle, forlorn, pure, unselfish and gallant." [62]

He stands for more than that. In his inevitable defeats, Quixote
triumphs over the monsters of his mind, answering the violence of
creation with a marvelously mad and willful violence of his own.
His battle is holy in the most profoundly human sense, for he knows
that man's existence is essentially sacred. He knows, as Eliade observed, that "The simple fact of *existing*, of *living in time*, can com-
prise a religious dimension." (Eliade's italics).[63]

This goes to the root of the matter. If we lose sight of this deep
knowledge, we lose our sense of life as the dynamic tension between love and strife that ennobled Don Quixote. In a world which
no longer offered him the mythological rewards of chivalry, he had
to invent "situations of the greatest peril such as would redound to
the eternal glory of his name." [64]

\*　\*　\*

The tension between love and strife is nowhere more naked than
in the puritan soul of the Marquis de Sade. In vehement reaction
against Rousseau's claim that man is born free but ends up culturally enchained, Sade reached deep into the violence that powers the
human heart in its most natural condition. Driven by the drastic
honesty of his mad mind beyond the bounds of what civilized society called sanity, Sade looked destiny's demons straight in the eye.

"Why is it, Messieurs... that in this world there are men whose
hearts have been so numbed, whose sentiments of honor and delicacy have been so deadened, that one sees them pleased and amused
by what degrades and soils them?" asks Duclos, the brilliant and
lascivious female narrator of *The 120 Days of Sodom*.[65] For such
alienated souls joy can be mined nowhere save from the depths of
degradation, Duclos observes.

A ferocious sexuality is the violent creativity Sade's heroes and
heroines employ to penetrate their numbness. They feel that only
an extreme eroticism can challenge the hell of human nature. Their
cry, "Ravish me!" becomes a direct provocation. One of Sade's insa-
tiably lecherous women goes so far as to advocate murder as an
erotic extravagance, for, she says, human beings reach the final par-
oxysm of delight only through an access of rage. As William Blake,

Sade's English contemporary, put it, "The tygers of wrath are wiser than the horses of instruction." [66]

At times, Sade's radical vision is lightened by a weird, self-mocking hilarity. Amid all the frantic perversions and raging couplings in *Sodom*, Sade lists a recipe for eating a piping hot omelette served on the naked buttocks of a girl bound belly-down upon a dining table. To eat the tasty dish, Sade recommends the use of an exceedingly sharp fork. In another scenario, he suggests covering a naked girl with honey, tying her to a column and letting her be attacked by a swarm of big flies.

Going one better than Sade, Heinrich Von Kleist fused natural and human furies in his early nineteenth century story, *The Earthquake in Chile*. The first sentence reads: "In Santiago, the capital of the kingdom of Chile, at the very moment of the great earthquake of 1647 in which many thousands of lives were lost, a young Spaniard by the name of Jeronimo Rugera, who had been locked up on a criminal charge, was standing against a prison pillar, about to hang himself." [67]

The earth itself is under threat, and "the greater part of the city suddenly collapsed with a roar, as if the firmament had given way, burying every living thing in its ruins." [68] Jeronimo searches the ruins for his paramour Josepha and their bastard child, and finds her, only to see her murdered by a crazed, self-righteous mob that blames the catastrophe on the sinners. "Here, murder me, you bloodthirsty tigers!" [69] Josepha shrieks as she's felled with a blow from a club. A child, mistakenly believed to be her bastard, has its brains bashed out against a wall, and Jeronimo is killed by his own father.

Thomas Mann described Kleist's story as being charged with "the archaic shudder of myth." Mann added that "Kleist knows how to put us on the rack and - such is his triumph as an artist - succeeds in making us thank him for that torture." [70]

The archaic shudder of myth shivers through the magnificent struggle Herman Melville's Captain Ahab wages with eternity. Out of a new country, confronting its own fresh strife with nature and human nature, comes a new tragic figure.

Ahab commands the Pequod in his search for Moby-Dick, a sperm whale of "uncommon magnitude and malignity," the white sea-monster of his soul. The captain is "a grand, ungodly, god-like man," his face scarred "not in the fury of any mortal fray, but an elemental strife at sea."[71] Ahab's soul is tainted by a sense of pride courting annihilation in the struggle to be human. Obsessed by his quenchless feud with the ocean itself, and with the demented brutality of the whale hunt, he says he'd strike the sun if it insulted him.

Ahab's challenge to fate leads to the loss of his ship, "which would not sink to hell until she had dragged down a living part of heaven." Watching the Pequod founder under the whale's attack, Ahab cries: "Oh now I feel my topmost greatness lies in my topmost grief... For hate's sake I spit my last breath at thee."[72] Strangled by the harpoon's flying line, Ahab is sucked down into the depths of the ocean attached to the beast he has hunted all his life. The captain gives his life for hate's sake, but it's a tonic hatred, a profoundly human hatred of a murderous eternity symbolized by the giant whale that kills him, an eternity that executes every man in the end.

An essentially modern ambivalence charges the thrust of Ahab's struggle with the whale. On the one hand, Ahab's fury with the elements suggests a fundamental antagonism between man and the gods of nature; a fight to the death that can only end when one or other of these antagonists is swallowed by the sea. Yet in *Moby-Dick* one senses an undertone of Kant's suggestion that nature deliberately wills discord, so that man may be impelled to a new exertion of his powers, and to the further development of his natural capacities. In this view, nature, far from simply being a ferocious foe, a source of savagery and terrible caprice, becomes a fresh bounty of challenges for humanity's fighting spirit.

In Ahab's century it seemed necessary to many passionate minds that God, at once man's most powerful enemy and his most profound spiritual concept, had to be terminated once and for all. This was necessary if a moral universe deriving its authority from humanity alone were to be established on earth. If eternity itself could not be killed, at least its figurehead could be.

The killing of God was a marvelously bold act of creative violence, as daring in its way as the original invention of a Supreme Deity who conjured up a world out of the void and gave it purpose. By murdering God, man became responsible for his own meanings in a world of his own making.

These modern, would-be God-killers tried many strategies, from intellectual argument to raw contempt. Deicide was seen as a cool imperative or a fervent necessity; but in the end the weapon that actually cut the Supreme Being's throat was a kind of guilty laughter.

Nietzsche, the boldest assassin, imagined a scene in which mad Zarathustra runs through a market place with a lantern crying out that he is looking for God. "Have you lost him then?" bystanders ask. "Is he hiding, has he emigrated?" [73] "We've killed him," the lunatic retorts, "we're all his murderers." Yet we, the deicides, can admire the god-killers among us, Nietzsche says. We can "love the great despisers because they are the great adorers, they are arrows of longing for the other shore." [74] What can be loved in man, Nietzsche adds, is that he is a transition and a destruction.

*　　*　　*

After Ahab's grand hatred, literary tragedy was infected by a radical desperation. What Dostoevsky called "this strange disease of modern life" [75] added a dimension of anguished self-wounding to the desire for a kind of bleak self-knowledge, an insight leading nowhere but to an absolute despair.

This strange disease runs rampant in Dostoyevsky's Russians. Raskolnikov murders an old woman with an axe, and his true life of feeling begins. In *The Brothers Karamazov*, a young girl deliberately slams a door on her hand and a young man lets a vicious child bite his finger to the bone. Dmitri, the wildest of the Karamazov brothers - "the lowest reptile," by his own admission - seeks the vilest and most violent degradation with a kind of crazed joy. "And in the very depths of that degradation I begin a hymn of praise," he cries; for "What to the mind is shameful, is beauty and nothing else to the heart." [76]

Dmitri conjures up echoes of Oedipus when he cries out from the depths of his despair: "I understand now that men such as I need a blow, a blow of destiny." [77] Like Oedipus, he accepts the blame for his father's murder, though in his case he is guilty by intent, if not by deed. He willingly suffers the torture of accusation and public shame, hoping for purification. But Dmitri is only momentarily purified; the ritual Christian repentance doesn't really take root in his hot heart. "What a thirst for existence and consciousness has sprung up in me within these peeling walls," he tells his saintly younger brother, when Alyosha visits him in prison. "I think I could stand anything, any suffering, only to be able to repeat to myself every moment, *I exist!*' [78] Despite his very modern despair, Dmitri, in his own humble yet rebellious fashion, repeats humanity's basic question: Should a man just lie down and take the blows of Fate? Or should he not risk everything just to say, with a defiant pride that might cost him his life: *I exist!*

The last literary figure to date to display such defiant pride is Joseph Conrad's Kurtz, in *Heart of Darkness*. Kurtz's furious ambition is brutal, it is terminal; yet it is also a creatively violent response to a creation symbolized by the steamy world of an Africa that, in the early 1900s, was still, for white minds, haunted by savagery.

Conrad's narrator, Marlow, penetrates the interior of that imagined darkness, and finds Kurtz dying amidst his attempt to build a personal kingdom on the backs of the natives. His house is guarded by severed and blackened heads on stakes, as if he were the prince of a ruined cannibal empire. "He had kicked himself loose of the earth... had kicked the very earth to pieces," [79] Marlow says. Kurtz curses the eternal jungle, much as Ahab damned the sea. His powerful voice fades out in that famous final whisper, *The horror! The horror!*

Kurtz's horror is not only a revulsion against his own descent into savagery; more poignantly, it expresses the torment of a man who has stared straight into the eye of eternity - an eternity mankind must always have the courage to assault. It takes a great heart to challenge a black fate; Kurtz had that heart, and it burst in the struggle. Like Ahab, his topmost greatness lay in his topmost grief. With Kurtz's tormented whisper went the last attempt in our time to confront the violence of creation with the proud violence of the human spirit. "What a loss to me - to us! ... To the world," [80] Kurtz's fiancee says to Marlow.

There are many and complex reasons why such radical confrontations with eternity appear to have lapsed. There is, most forcefully, the overwhelming pressure of a truly murderous tide of destructive violence in our time, epitomized by Hiroshima and Auschwitz. Such brutal events have undermined our confidence and sapped our spirits, eroding our old faith that we can challenge heaven and hell. Perhaps, as Malraux remarked, Western civilization has simply lost faith in its own credentials. In this depleted condition we seem to have mislaid our basic belief, dating back to Homer, that our cultural energy has the power to integrate and transform any human situation, no matter how terrible.

Or maybe it's the other way around. Perhaps our shaky confidence has undercut the kind of courage we need to transmute the destructive power of raw violence. Maybe it's this very lack of valor that has opened the way for cataracts of unrestrained catastrophe. Altogether, we seem to have lost our cosmic kind of bravery and no longer love life despite its terrors, like Oedipus or Job. Or Kurtz, who, at the moment of his death, "lived his years again in every detail of desire, temptation, and surrender." [81]

Nature abhors a vacuum, and the emptied space we once filled with such verve and high courage has been claimed by death. Death is a master from Germany, Celan wrote in his bleak poem, *Death Fugue,* [82] and the Germany he names is a country we all seem to inhabit in this century.

In this context, art can only confront us with a frenzied honesty of horror; with Kurtz's desolation, but without his proud response. Nowadays, art's violence is no longer fruitful; it is merely mournful, desperate or shocking. "I had not thought death had undone so many," [83] says the narrator in T.S. Eliot's *The Wasteland.* "That corpse you planted last year in your garden,/Has it begun to sprout?'" [84]

In a perverse parody of creative violence, Camus' Caligula commits terrible acts to find out if anything really changes, and makes the discovery that nothing ever does. People are surprised and frightened, but the sun sets as usual in the west. If you were given the power, Caligula says, if you had the courage, if you loved life, you would see this monster or this angel that you carry within yourselves break loose. [85]

The prime literary monster-angel of the period between the two world wars was the French novelist Louis-Ferdinand Celine. Celine's two great books, *Voyage to the End of Night* and *Death on the Installment Plan,* published in the 1930s, record the sentimental education of a young man in the emotional, physical and spiritual tumult of twentieth century history. Celine's savage, staccato style - a slangy French argot fired with all the ferocity of the street - contains the shriek of hatred, the howl of half-tamed demons, the yell of a savage joy.

*Death on the Installment Plan* covers the first eighteen years in the life of a boy born into genteel but harsh poverty in a Paris slum. The events in young Ferdinand's life in this overcharged and fabulous novel follow closely on Celine's own, but the book is a hallucination and a hell. It renders the boy's purgatory in being caught between a hysterical failure of a father and a limping, nagging martyr of a mother. Hunger, abuse and humiliation are breakfast lunch and dinner for young Ferdinand.

Beyond the miserable alley where Ferdinand lives lies a world of pimps, cutthroats, whores and swindlers, salted by the presence of one genius, the brilliantly deranged scientist-balloonist Des Pereires. Celine's account of Ferdinand's struggle to get hold of Des Pereires' frozen, shotgun-blasted remains after his master's suicide is a masterpiece of gut-churning yet hilarious horror. (The staccato, dotted connections that follow are Celine's.)

"I pull on the head...It wouldn't come loose...We weren't getting anywhere...It was stuck too solid...Especially the ears were welded fast...The whole thing made a solid block with the ice and the gravel...We could have unfastened the trunk and the legs by pulling hard enough...But not the head... the hash...It was one solid brick with the stones on the road...It couldn't be done...The body bent crooked like a Z... the head impaled on the gun barrel..." [86] This frozen, earthbound image of Des Pereires is a tragic contrast to the airy ascensions he enjoyed in his balloon.

Celine's prose marries paranoia with violence in an art of barbaric reality. *Death on the Installment Plan* has an affinity with Van Gogh's canvas, *Cornfield with Crows*. In both, a terrible lucidity is fused with a wild gaiety, enacting a uniquely modern nuptial of passionate terror and terrified passion. Celine's Des Pereires is Don Quixote seen through the prism of Sade's Sodom and Goya's depiction of Saturn devouring one of his children. But the child Celine's Saturn devours is his own soul. Man has become a self-consuming cannibal in an existential desert in which, as Stendhal remarked, God's only excuse is that he doesn't exist.

Perhaps the central image of our time is Kafka's helpless victim in *The Penal Colony*, a man having his crime written in blood on his flesh by a diabolical mechanical contraption; a crime whose accusation he can't even decipher. A twin image is Kafka's Gregor Samsa, who wakes up one morning to find he has turned into a bug. Looking down at his insect belly, Gregor asks, for all of us: "What has happened to me?" [87] The human bug he has become reduces Samsa to the level of a humanity fused with insectness, harking back to the psychical condition of early man struggling to define himself against the overwhelming presence of nature.

"What are the possibilities for man in the trap the world has become?" [88] Milan Kundera asks. He goes on: "The time was past when man had only the monster of his own soul to grapple with, the peaceful time of Joyce and Proust. In the novels of Kafka, Hasek, Musil, Broch, the monster comes from outside and is called *History*...impersonal, uncontrollable, incalculable, incomprehensible - and...inescapable."

Fate, now embodied as History, is a kind of epidemic, a sickness of the soul, a fatal disease of the spirit, and for many writers, a fever of raw, untransforming violence is the only means to create an antidote to such contagion.

Antonin Artaud, in his 1936 vision of a "Theatre of Cruelty," calls for a dramatic treatment to meet the ravages of this mortally infectious condition. "The theatre, like the plague, is a delirium," [89] Artaud declares. He envisages a spectacle of gestures and signs, a dramatic catharsis of "Cries, groans, apparitions, surprises...sudden changes of lights ... masks, effigies yards high... a violent exteriorization of cruelty..." A theatre that repudiates words for sounds, rhythms, silences, dreams and nightmares. "Let words be heard in their sonority rather than be exclusively taken for what they mean grammatically," [90] Artaud declares. Players and spectators alike shriek, scream, and act out their frenzies in a kind of extreme therapy that exorcizes their alienation and reconnects them with themselves. It is a theatre of emotional ferocity, a last, desperate attempt to purge the audience of its spiritual plague.

Artaud's strategy both parallels and challenges the Epic Theatre of Bertolt Brecht. Like Artaud, Brecht is outraged by an audience that History seems to have stunned and distanced from its dreams and nightmares. "True, their eyes are open, but they stare rather than see, just as they listen rather than hear," he says. "They look at the stage as if in a trance...a cowed, credulous, hypnotized mass." [91] The conventional strategies of dramatic empathy, in which actors attempt to become the characters they play, puts people's minds and hearts to sleep.

The weapon Brecht seizes to startle spectators from their trance is alienation itself. The audience must always be alert, aware that actors are acting a part, not attempting to be the people they portray. Coleridge's famous "willing suspension of disbelief" is denounced, to be replaced by a "state of suspicious inquiry." Brecht's

Alienation Effect "is one that allows us to recognize its subject, but at the same time makes it seem unfamiliar."

If the verdict on an actor's performance is "he didn't act Lear, he was Lear," the man is to be hounded from the stage. Mocking Aristotle's notion of tragic pleasure, Brecht says of his audience: "Let us hope that their theatre may allow them to enjoy as entertainment...the terror of their unceasing transformation." [92]

In the aftermath of Auschwitz and Hiroshima, the literary arts of so many cultures increasingly call upon crude violence to kick-start creativity. All the categories of literary endeavor, including poetry, fiction and drama, and on to popular novels and science fiction, comic books and childrens' literature are supercharged with overheated, disheartening furies.

Under such pressure the literary imagination appears to sputter. The power to reimagine things, to reinvent the world out of the whole cloth of one's invention and perception seems clogged by the ceaseless disturbance charging everyday political and social events. The monster of History, "impersonal, uncontrollable, incalculable, incomprehensible - and...inescapable," sucks the fuel from the imagination of contemporary authors, no matter what brutal frenzies their words conjure. "No longer a mere chronicle of events, it [history] was becoming an anxious scrutiny of the past for any light it might cast on the dark vista of the future," Andre Malraux commented. "Western culture was losing faith in itself." [93]

The present plague of the spirit turns men into mocking murderers of themselves. The eponymous hero of Samuel Beckett's novel *Murphy* comes to a self-inflicted end. Before lighting a candle in a room filled with gas, Murphy pens a note requesting that his ashes be flushed down the toilet of Dublin's Abbey Theatre. But Murphy's ashes meet a silly fate; they are accidentally spilled over the floor of a pub and swept out with the trash.

In *The Unnamable* Beckett mimics Calderon's famous line about the sin of having been born: "I'm looking for my mother to kill her, I should have thought of that a bit earlier, before being born." But, as Estragon says in *Waiting for Godot,* "We always find something, eh, Didi, to give us the impression that we exist?

In this plaintive query we hear faint echoes across the centuries of Job's pained cry: "What is man, that thou shouldest...try him every moment?" But the cry is weak now, and the force of a tragic response such as Job's seems to exceed our numbed spirits. We have to ask: Has eternity finally killed us?

Whether or no, it's been a while since Captain Ahab burst his heart in battle with the white whale, and our next true tragic hero may be a very long time coming.

# 3
# the marriage
# of terror & rapture

A circle of Stone Age men and women sit around
a fire in a dark cave listening to the sharp high notes
of a bone flute. The flute, made from the hollowed
leg bone of a large bird, expresses a plangent longing.

Soon, other musicians add their tonal accents.
Some blow one-holed, bird-bone whistles, others
clatter castanets made from ibex vertebrae, scrape
rasps shaped from the toothed jawbone of a mammoth, shake rattles carved from the ivory of wild
boar tusks. One player bangs a drum of mammoth
vertebrae with mallets made from reindeer antlers,
another tinkles a simple xylophone created from
stone stalagmites and stalactites broken from the
cave floor and ceiling. The hoarse shriek of predatory eagles, the thunder of bison hooves, the trumpeting of mammoths, the hiss of crocodiles, the
grunt of a mountain lion echo through the strong
rhythms. Those in the circle who aren't playing instruments clap their hands and chant. Beyond the
firelight circle the surrounding darkness is charged
with natural and supernatural powers which both
threaten and thrill the huddled human beings.

The flute player sets the melody while the other

*instruments elaborate the melodic line. The flute leads because its mythical properties are derived from the bird from whose leg bone it has been fashioned - birds being regarded as magical animals traveling between land and sky, earth and heaven. The instrument is played by a man or woman with special qualities, one whose spirit moves through the mist separating the assembled men and women from the potent, enveloping otherness of life.*

*As the flames flicker down to hot coals, the pace of the music quickens. The drummer's mallet blurs as the beat quickens. All sound merges into a single throb, an agitated repetition of one short sequence of notes, charging the pulse of everyone circling the camp fire. Bodies jerk and sway, as if in a fit. The quick, angry rhythm has a life of its own, swifter than a hummingbird's wings, harsher than a buzzard's shriek.*

*Suddenly, the fluteplayer begins to sing. He opens his throat and releases a single, sharp note. The sound is hardly human, echoing a hawk's high screech heard way above the earth. The singer's eyes roll up into his skull, his face is twisted in a hideous grimace, his body possessed by ecstatic twitches and shudders linked to the instrumental cadence. Struggling to keep pace with the singer's leaping song, his fellow musicians fire up the harmony to an almost unbearable pitch. Others in the firelit band rise, link arms, and begin to dance, stamping in time to the rapid drumming, their ghostly shadows flickering on the rough stone walls, their feet following the small hollows in the stone floor of the cave made by generations of dancers.*

*All at once the singer ceases. He falls into a deep trance. His body sags like an empty sack. The musicians stop playing, except for one drummer, who taps out a soft tattoo, a sort of last post for a soul journeying in strange realms. When the coals are dim and the singer opens his eyes again on the*

35

*world within the cave, all present know he has*
*touched the violence of creation and survived the*
*powerful experience with the force of his song, con-*
*summating the marriage of terror and rapture that*
*is the primal human experience.*

\*    \*    \*

A Paleolithic orchestra such as this must have performed its wild music in many a Stone Age cavern. Such ecstatic playing, singing, and dancing expressed our ancestors' vivid sense of being at once in and out of nature; a nature whose turbulent powers threatened man's very survival while inspiring the magic of his dreams. Rapturous chanting generated the entranced state which gave access to a direct apprehension of the terrible beauty of life.

This primal musical purpose continues today, in a wide variety of forms. For example, the word for "sing" in the language of the Selk'nam peoples of Tierra del Fuego signifies falling into a trance. Surrounded by a perceived reality in which all living and inanimate things are charged with spirit, the Selk'nam, like many other native peoples of America, Africa, Asia and Australasia, use chanting to engage dangerous natural powers, propitiate threatening presences, cure sickness, cast love spells and ease pain. In a number of still vibrant cultures shamans use such "power songs" to battle demons and guide their patients through the thickets of the supernatural.

Hand pianos, xylophones, pan pipes, drums vie with one another in the *vimbuza* spirit possession dance of the Zambian Tumbuka and the Yewe cult festivals of Togo and southern Ghana. Yewe, the god of thunder and lightning, is served by a secret society whose ceremonies arouse feelings of profound awe which can only be exorcised by a ritual named *wuxexele*, in which the deity is honored by clapping, singing, the shaking of rattles, the clanging of bells and frenetic drumming. These ceremonies create a furious melodic ambiance in which people, gods and demons all commune. There's a deep connection here with the derivation of the word "tragedy" from the Greek *tragoidia*, which Virgil translated as "goat song," linked to the randy animal associated with the cult of wine and its drunken demi-god, Dionysus.

Such musical intensities are not limited to so-called "primitive" societies. They also electrify some contemporary cultures marked by a high degree of social and melodic sophistication.

In the music of Indonesia, for instance, musical and physical violence runs rampant. Singers in the Sumatran *dabus* ceremony achieve an ecstasy in which they can walk on broken glass and wrap red hot chains around their necks, with no apparent ill effects. Similarly, the Balinese *Calonarang* acts out the turbulent struggle between the benign mythical animal Barong and the evil witch Rangda. Barong's musical assistants, carried away in a demonic possession, perform a dangerous stabbing dance with their *kris* daggers.

The ancient union of terror and bliss is more subtly expressed in the complex harmonies of Indian music. Improvisation, the heart of the Indian musical expression, builds an inventive anarchy into the texture of its tradition. In the classical Hindustani musical culture, developed in the northern half of the subcontinent, a single melodic line is plucked out on the lute-like *sitar* and *sarod*, counterpointed by the rapid heartbeat of the *tabla* drum. This melodic *raga* provides the armature for great flights of fancy responding to the hour of the day, the feeling of the season, or maybe the player's emotional state of mind. Abrupt shifts of speed, clashes between the basic melody and the performer's impromptu inspiration, create a harmonious anarchy, voicing a sentiment expressed in the ancient Sanskrit *Bhagavadgita*, in a dialogue between Krishna and Arjuna: "Equate pain and pleasure, profit and loss, victory and defeat. And fight! There is no blame this way." [94]

Like Hindustani harmonics, Western music evolved a dynamic tension between dread and enchantment; between rhythms conjuring up the dark powers of gods and demons and others striving to celebrate an Olympian serenity.

In the old Hellenic world, the gods Apollo and Dionysus symbolized this tense opposition, and each deity was served by a favored instrument that best expressed his character. The seven-string Greek lyre, shaped like a pair of curved antlers, was the servant of Apollo, god of light, truth and healing. The plucking of Apollo's golden lyre accompanied the Homeric epics; it was, at best, the instrument of a profound meditation upon the glories and mysteries of being.

Dionysus, on the other hand, engendered a savage music on the *aulos flute*, an instrument whose reedy, plaintive melodies mimicked human longing and despair yet could also soar to dithyrambs of orgiastic ecstasy. Singing and dancing themselves to exhaustion, devotees of the Dionysiac cult purged their terrors in a release at once emotional, sexual and spiritual.

Sex and violence, "our two main avenues to the sacred," [95] gave Dionysus his power; the demi-god epitomized "those animal powers that both manifest our finest energies and threaten to devastate all that we cherish. If you let him into your life, under appropriately ritualized circumstances, you will be deeply disturbed but also deeply enlivened, touched by the sources of good and evil and yet sanely returned to the casual comedy of civil society. If you refuse him entry he will invade, and you will die one of the many deaths he mischievously conceives in his elaborate theater of the mad." [96]

Dionysus, who could turn into a lion, a panther, or a bull whenever he pleased, presided over the Spring Festivals, when all the trees burst into bud and the whole world seemed intoxicated with desire. In the demi-deity's flashing tunes, wild dance and hectic song, the reveller's spirit seemed to leave his body and become momentarily divine and ecstatically potent, much like the Stone Age flute-player in his cave.

Finally, in the Orphic movement of the sixth century BC, the Dionysian and Apollonian cults began to fuse. The lyre and the flute played in harmony, to honor the gods and compose paeans to their fierce glory, as in this Orphic hymn to Zeus:

> *Thou ruler of the sea, the sky and vast abyss,*
> *Thou who shatterest the heavens with Thy thunder peals;*
> *Thou before whom spirits fall in awe, and gods do tremble;*
> *Thou to whom the fates belong, so wise, so unrelenting Thou;*
> *Draw near and shine in us.* [97]

The Orphic opposition between Apollonian and Dionysian modes was profoundly fruitful, providing a strong structure for the Western musical tradition while also spurring the development of new art form: dramatic tragedy. Orphic song celebrated nature's violent energies within a civilized framework that honored their original vitality.

However, the Orphic synthesis unravelled after Greece and Rome's decline. In medieval Europe Apollo's grave serenities were subsumed by the monotonous solemnities of Christian plainsong while the lively tempo of the Dionysian dithyramb was carried through towns and villages by troubadours and French jongleurs;

by traveling minstrels and the students called goliards; by the "scops" and "gleemen" of England; by Welsh, Scottish and Irish bards; by the Scalds of Scandinavia and Iceland and the Gaukler and Minnesinger of Germany. The minstrels rattled drums, whistled through flutes, juggled, danced and performed magic tricks, celebrating every secular delight, from chivalrous love to bawdy fun - a subversive jollity that provoked John Milton to complain that the Devil seemed to have all the good tunes.

There was another, more gruesome sense in which the Devil had the tunes: the terrible Dance of Death. A reaction to the ravages of the bubonic plague that decimated Europe in the thirteenth and fourteenth centuries, this wild phenomenon was also a protest against the failure of the spiritual power of the Church and the temporal authority of the ruling nobility to protect common folk from the hideous affliction. In reaction, a papal resolution decreed that "Whoever buries the dead should do so with fear, trembling and decency. No one shall be permitted to sing Devil songs and perform games and dances which are inspired by the Devil."

The Devil was a very busy choreographer during the Black Death. At his urging, entire communities were infected by a dementia that sent crowds cavorting through European villages and towns for days on end, until they collapsed and died. Men and women were goaded by Luciferian visions to leap wildly into the air, in market places, churches and even their own homes, howling out the names of demons, screaming for death to release them from their torments, "tearing their cheeks, their hair, their breasts in agony, because they see Hell through the prison-bars and hear the raging of its fiends, and feel the clasp upon their wrists and ankles of clawed hairy demon hands." [98]

The Dance of Death was a purgation of despair, an attempt to ease the pressure on the spirit of terrifying realities that had no other remedy. Its raw violence offered a momentary liberation, the transient but exhilarating defiance of a cruel fate. Skirting the edge of the abyss, these demented dancers found a brief release from the horrors of an extreme condition.

Not only the plague caused people to cavort so crazily. The Italian folk dance, the tarantella, was said to be induced by the bite of a tarantula. A sect called the Chorisants extracted money from choreomaniacs by claiming it could cure the affliction by trampling on the bodies of exhausted dancers. Such delirious "Choremania" recalled the Corybantic dancing orgies of ancient Greece, where the Maenads of Dionysus could get so carried away with the sheer ecstasy of movement that they were capable of tearing spectators limb from limb. The tarantella, and other such outbursts, were a reversion to a primitive condition, before the musical energies of untamed violence were integrated into an Orphic fusion of terror and rapture.

*    *    *

The Orphic spirit did not die with the eclipse of classical Greece. Some two thousand years later its spirit was still strong in Mozart, and one of the most expressive musical unions of the fearful and the sublime is found in his opera, *Don Giovanni.*

The central figure of *Don Giovanni* is a decadent Spanish aristocrat, a Don Juan who seduces hundreds of women to serve his voracious vanity. The emotional terrorism charging the act of seduction is more important to this Don Juan than the pleasures of dalliance. He's a driven man, a character pursuing a radical urge for freedom even at the cost of private decency or public good. He destroys the old world of authority and order, embodied in the dark figure of the Commendatore, whom he kills in a duel. But the old world comes back to haunt him. In a shivering scene the statue raised to the memory of the Commendatore knocks at his door. Don Giovanni is shaken to his roots, but he refuses to do penance. Night falls and flames shoot up from the trembling earth. Invisible spirits raise terrifying voices as they surround the Don and carry him down to hell.

In the figure of the Don, Mozart created a complex character, one who is both hero and villain. He is a modern man, impelled to express his own passions, to break all the rules, even if his actions destroy all social order. Spurred by a sensual urge to live and love, to conquer and enjoy, his willingness to risk everything is his dangerous, even fatal, life-force. The music is by turns savage and gentle, shouting and whispering; the brass blares and violins ripple. The Don's descent to damnation is expressed by rude yet majestic trombones symbolizing the supernatural power of the Commendatore. But the harsh and solemn sounds of his fall into hell are followed by a lighthearted epilogue derived from the Italianate *opera buffa* popular in Mozart's day. This abrupt switch of mood, from sepulchral trombones to *buffo* jollity, is one of the boldest transitions in operatic history. Like William Blake, his near contemporary, Mozart knew that without contraries there is no progression; that the electric tension between existential fury and passionate exhilaration sparks all new life.

After Mozart, a new force emerged in European music: the figure of the composer as hero. These valiant, free-spirited artists reached down into the most ancient sources of musical expression, seeking to rediscover the potency and verve of the ancient coupling of anguish and rejoicing.

The first towering artist-hero in this mold was Ludwig van Beethoven. That big, clumsy "unlicked bear" [99] of a man disdained musical conventions at will. When small-minded folk told him he had done things that simply weren't permitted, he grandly retorted, "Then *I* permit them." [100]

There was much of Herman Melville's Captain Ahab in Beethoven's character. Like Ahab, he harbored a fury potent enough to confront creation. Like Ahab, he saw himself as God's Lieutenant, willing to strike the sun itself if it insulted him. "I shall seize Fate by the throat," Beethoven declared. "It shall never wholly subdue me." [101] In the last moments of his life he shook his fist at heaven.

This sense of a cosmic challenge suffuses Beethoven's Third Symphony, the *Eroica.* The music is a great soul's battle with the agony and ecstasy of the human condition. The first movement, opening with furious hammer blows, declares a defiance. The melodic themes continue the conflict as dissonance piles upon dissonance, until the whole orchestra becomes one giant instrument of percussion, screeching and shouting, brassy and disruptive. The horns fight the strings and harmonies compete to achieve the glorious joyfulness that found its purest expression in his famous ninth symphony ode.

Though originally dedicated to Napoleon, Beethoven's own heroic struggle with Fate was the true theme of the *Eroica.* The fierce battle Beethoven fought to preserve his sanity and his love of life against illness and despair was, in his mind, also a fight for Europe's fate. Beethoven was Europe, his soul was hers, dependent on his capacity to provoke heaven. For Beethoven, the artist was Prometheus bringing the gift of fire, stolen from the gods, to mankind.

Beethoven gave voice to his personal struggle more intimately in the *Moonlight Sonata*. The lullaby calm of the prelude, and the dreamy minuet of the interlude that follows, is tested by a tempest of sound in the last movement, a rhetorical coda of seething scales and arpeggios. However, by the end of the composition the tension between his soul's delight and his passion's fury is resolved by a rare tranquility of spirit.

Richard Wagner upstaged even Beethoven as a world-shaking artist-hero. For Wagner, raging passion became a mythological axe, a blade to cut fate's throat. "We two, the world and I, are stubborn fellows at loggerheads, and naturally whichever has the thinner skull will get it broken," [102] the young composer declared.

*Tristan and Isolde*, Wagner's most personal opera, equates a legendary love triangle with his own desire for Mathilde Wesendonck, the wife of a devoted disciple. In the old chronicle, the Cornish knight Tristan kills the fiance of Isolde, the daughter of the King of Ireland, and becomes her secret, illicit lover. To escape their hopeless situation, they agree to die, believing they will meet and be free to love in heaven. Isolde gives Tristan a goblet containing a potion they both mistakenly believe is a mortal poison. The couple share the drug, enjoy a night of tremendous passion, and survive. Next day, however, Tristan is mortally wounded by one of Isolde's father's knights, and she dies of grief as he expires in her arms.

The opera's music is intensely chromatic, charged with color and contrast, almost narcotic in the liquid vibrancy of its chords. The succession of dissonant harmonic tensions, the fight for expression between the lonely singers and a powerful orchestra, generates an orgy of the emotions, a feast of yearning and frustration. Death is love's resolution, a terrible paradox that somehow becomes a triumph, as in the story of Romeo and Juliet. "Love, excited by the arts of sorcery to the highest pitch of erotic rapture, seeks only to gratify itself, reckless of all consequences," [103] is how Gustav Kobbe, Wagner's first biographer, expressed it.

According to Denis de Rougemont, Tristan and Iseult is a fable which "operates wherever passion is dreamed of as an ideal instead of being feared like a malignant fever; wherever its fatal character is welcomed, invoked or imaged as a magnificent and desirable disaster instead of as simply a disaster." [104] De Rougemont continues: "Why does Western Man wish to suffer this passion which lacerates him and which all his common sense rejects? Why does he yearn after this particular kind of love, notwithstanding that its effulgence must coincide with his self-destruction? The answer is that he reaches self-awareness and tests himself only by risking life - in suffering and on the verge of death."

After Wagner, European art searched for fresh sources of vitality. It reached outward to "primitive" cultures, and inward to its ancient origins, seeking a vivid savagery to cut away the decadence of established forms in art, music, dance and architecture. "What are needed now are barbarians," Andre Gide declared in 1911; barbarians allied with "those half-tamed demons that inhabit the human breast." [105] Recognizing the artistic cultures of Africa and Oceania, European artists sought to reconnect with the intuitive primitivism in themselves, to marry violence with rejoicing in fresh ways.

One of the most influential acts in this cultural upheaval was Stravinsky's ballet, *The Rite of Spring* - a musical pandemonium, a wild devil dance, a dive deep into the collective unconscious of the human race. In 1913 Vaslav Nijinsky's presentation of the work in Paris shocked the audience with the savage power and supercharged contortions of the dancers. Shivering, shaking, jerking, jumping, they acted out the fierce ritual of the annual rebirth of Nature's generative energies.

"I recall Marie Plitz, calmly facing a hooting audience, whose violence completely drowned out the orchestra," wrote the contemporary French critic, Andre Levinson. "She seemed to dream, her knees turned inward, the heels pointing out - inert. A sudden spasm shook her body out of its corpse-like rigor. At the fierce onward thrust of the rhythm, she trembled in ecstatic, irregular jerks. This primitive hysteria, terribly burlesque as it was, completely caught and overwhelmed the spectator." [106]

Nijinsky's provocative presentation of Stravinsky's *Rite of Spring* made common ground with early experiments in what came to be called modern dance. In a rebellion against the stereotyped choreography of the classical ballet, these dancers sought a more expressive form, a freedom to be wild in an access of original energy. Emphasis was placed on the human body in its most extreme emotions, rather than on the formalized movements that control the traditional corps de ballet. In modern dance, the performer is vulnerable to the world, naked and unmasked. Body and limbs become flexible, free to be racked, twisted and dragged across the stage. The dance draws its force from a direct connection to the shock of the human condition, filtered through a screen of the performer's technique. Its disciplined anarchy magically transforms the primal power of violence into images of wild delight.

\* \* \*

In the cave of Lascaux in south-western France, in the section known as the Shaft - the deepest, darkest hole in the subterranean labyrinth - is a scene painted around 17,000 years ago: a wounded bison charges a terrified hunter, who seems to have fallen over backward in fright. Rendered in the round in rich ochre and black, the creature bristles with a fierce power. Despite the fact that its entrails are hanging out of a wound made by the hunter's spear thrust, the enraged animal's stance remains dense with menace. In contrast, the hunter, wearing nothing but a bird mask, is sketched as a stick man, flat and spindly-limbed, a mere diagram dominated by the bison's marvelous ferocity.

What is striking about this scene, as in many other Paleolithic cave paintings found in south-western France, northern Spain and the northern Sahara, is the way in which dangerous and energetic beasts had such a powerful effect upon the Stone Age artists' imagination. While mammoths, lions, woolly rhinoceroses, bison and wild horses crowd cave walls, the gentler prey these early humans hunted and depended upon for food - the reindeer, rabbits, aurochs, ibex and other edible animals, whose hides, bones and hair provided Paleolithic people with meat, implements, weapons and clothes - appear to have excited their interest far less forcefully. And man himself, in his own picture, is a mere cipher.

Archeologists, speaking of the recently discovered, 32,000-year-old paintings in the Grotte Chauvet in southern France, have remarked that, "Out of these people's whole bestiary, the artists chose predatory, dangerous animals." The Stone age painters attempted "to capture the essence" of the animals by painting species which symbolized danger, strength and power. [107]

It seems clear that the energies of the natural world, embodied in fierce and potent beasts, were at once a threat and an enchantment to Stone Age cave dwellers. Their art found a terrible beauty in such dangerous powers, and prehistoric painting appears to be less an exercise in sympathetic magic - the attempt to control prey by manipulating its images - than an instinctual grasp of the vital role of violence in a natural realm ruled by mysterious forces; a uniquely human impulse to acknowledge and transform that perception through a fusion of art and spirituality, a union of awed fright and naked enchantment.

The same sensibility informs an ancient carving found in Tequixquiac, Mexico. Dated around 10,000 BC, the carving conjures a wild coyote's face out of the pelvic sacrum of a domesticated llama. The coyote's eyes are dark sockets in the skull-like visage, the snarling snout is set to tear flesh; the erect, flint-cut ears seem to quiver with the excitement of an imminent kill. In this small art object (the head is barely seven inches wide) part of the skeleton of a humble beast of burden is transformed by a predator's dangerous power.

This skilfully carved coyote skull is the ancestor of many such transformations, from a variety of historical cultures. It foreshadows the dancing goat-men cavorting with horse-headed lions in a cylinder seal from ancient Ur, and the Sumerian limestone carving of a frightening half-woman, half leopard creature. Assyrian *lammasu*, the massive human-headed winged bulls that guarded the gates of ancient Khorsabad, express a similar sentiment, as do the Shang Dynasty's tiger-headed human monsters and bronze wine vessels, whose sides swarm with snakes and crocodiles. There is a bronze Etruscan she-wolf with copious, multiple teats and snarling fangs; the compact, glowing ferocity of a golden prowling panther from seventh century BC Scythia; a Han Dynasty tomb guarded by fabulous, evil-defying beasts; an Olmec jaguar mask and the plumed serpents of the pyramid at Teotihuacan. Later, we find demonic Gothic gargoyles, and the superb wooden guardians of the thirteenth century Shinto Todaiji Temple at Nara, whose glowering eyes, snarling lips, bared teeth, flaring eyebrows, tensed fists and swirling draperies artfully express the ultimate in demonic fury.

Describing the carved and painted ceremonial masks of the Pacific Northwest, the anthropologist Claude Levi-Strauss wrote of their simultaneously naive and ferocious mechanical contraptions, that can "cause mouths to mock a novice's terrors, eyes to mourn his death, beaks to devour him." [108] For the Kwakiutl and the Tlingit, the Haida and Tsimshian, such striking representations give entry to the fertile menace of the natural and supernatural world, and offer a exhilarating sense of sharing a forceful fate.

An artist's talent to transform the fertile energies of violence is superbly rendered in an eighth century AD Mayan lintel relief from Yaxchilan, in the Yucatan. In this limestone tableau, King Shield Jaguar, sporting the shrunken head of a sacrificial victim on his feathered crown, is shown holding a flaming torch over his kneeling wife, Lady Xoc. He pulls a cord knotted with thorns through her tongue, dripping her bright blood onto a scroll. By means of a symbolic yet marvelously delicate art, the lintel's carver manages to convey the couple's fears and hopes, their guilt and their arrogance, their sense of weakness and their thrill of life. Humanity's long struggle to marry existential terror with a passionate elan through the medium of art shines through this frozen scene, that would not be nearly so moving without the brisk touch of violence.

A similar quality enlivens a small Assyrian relief from Nimrud, dating from the early eighth century BC. A lioness mauls a Nubian boy, whose head is thrown back in helpless surrender, his throat offered to the beast. One of the lioness's forepaws supports the wounded child's swooning head, and the big cat's jaw seems simultaneously murderous and tender, with the hard-mouthed savagery of a predator and the soft-mouthed gentleness of a bitch lifting a pup.

The brutal aspects of this scene are transformed but not betrayed by the exquisite quality of the art and the beauty of the gold, red faience, and lapis lazuli that clothe the relief. There's a subtle empathy in these exquisite finishes, manifest in such details as the tiny, gilded ivory pegs that represent the boy's curly golden locks. The opulence of the materials and the sensitivity of the design transmute a violent act into a harmonious composition without weakening its original intensity.

This artful fugue of ferocity and harmony is epitomized in a superb fifteenth century porcelain vase from the Ming Dynasty. On the rounded surface of this twenty-two-inch masterpiece, a fierce dragon-serpent with cruel claws and bulging eyes is painted with a serene stylistic elegance. The rough menace of the dangerous creature is in tension with the sleek grace of the blue and white coloring. Fine materials and great skill serve to fuse fear with beauty; in this fusion, violence becomes graceful but never tame. Such superb works of art express a sensibility forged in a furnace that burns away the dross of self-pity, leaving a precious residue of earned exhilaration.

Art's capacity to effect a profoundly civilizing metamorphosis of violence shines through the fifth century BC marble pediment of the temple of Aphaia, on the Greek island of Aegina. In this tableau, a fallen warrior is shown lying with one arm supported by his shield. His face is grave as he stares death in the face; his last surge of life is concentrated in the bulging bicep that clings to the shield, but it's a strength that has spent its force. The pose is heroic, Homeric; but it also movingly expresses the brutal sacrifice war demands from its actors. The compassion this clearly evoked in the classical sculptor is validated by an implicit acceptance of the original severity that shines through his fellow feeling.

A similar tough empathy is manifest in the bronze statue of a dying Gaul from the Hellenic kingdom of Pergamon, in Asia Minor. Dated around 230 BC (but now seen in a later Roman copy of the lost original) it shows a naked warrior with a gaping, Christ-like wound in his side. The defeated enemy leans heavily on one hand, watching his life drain away; his wild hair and rough face point up the pathos of his passing. Even a hostile barbarian has an immortal spirit, the Greek artist recognized, one made all the more vivid by the agony of its mortal end. Several centuries later, on Trajan's triumphal column in Imperial Rome, the carvings of captive men, women and children express such sorrow the stone itself seems to weep.

The artistic impulse of fellow feeling conjured from violence was also extended to animals. In a panel of the fourth century BC Alexander Sarcophagus a hunter prepares to club a deer to death. The man jerks the deer's head back by the antlers, cruelly arching its throat, and the artist conveys both the hunter's proud triumph and the creature's natural fright. The dangle of the deer's forelegs, the gape of its mouth, the silent scream swelling its breast and the wild terror in its eye move the viewer's heart to sympathy with the agony of a living creature anticipating a brutal death. Similarly, a pebble mosaic from Pella, Greece, almost contemporaneous with the Sarcophagus, illustrates the fear of a stag and fawn cornered by two naked hunters and their hound. Though the hunters seem vulnerable in their nudity, their postures exhibit an arrogant assurance that points up the beasts' touching exposure.

*   *   *

A more modern instance of savagery transformed by art leaps out at us from Artemisia Gentileschi's 1620 painting, *Judith Slaying Holofernes*. A watershed in the long history of creative violence, *Judith Slaying Holofernes* strikes a startlingly contemporary note.

Holofernes's dark face, surprised in sleep, is frozen in terror while Judith and her maid go about their determined act of murder. As Judith's sword slices through the victim's neck, even as she bends away from the spurting blood, the expression on her face is pitiless, yet somehow sacramental.

This biblical scene, of the Jewess Judith decapitating the Assyrian general Holofernes to save her town from conquest, represented a Renaissance determination to resist tyranny. But the style is much more intense than this conventional symbolism warrants. Gentileschi's passion is so vehement that all the painter's skill, her brilliant chiaroscuro, can hardly contain it within the frame.

Under the guise of genre painting, this work introduces the theme of human ferocity without the cover of ritual. More significantly, it locates the theatre of transformation within the human body and soul, much as Shakespeare had done in *King Lear* fifteen years before, and Matthias Grunewald in his Isenheim altarpiece a century or so earlier. Gentileschi's secular tableau shows human beings acting out their primal drama in the flesh, and her vivid art makes it bearable for a civilized eye to view its own dark shadow. Where the act itself would have been too horrible to watch, the painting, shocking as it is, allows us to contemplate fundamental furies.

Gentileschi's canvas leads two centuries later straight to Francisco de Goya. His work marks the full-fledged emergence of art as outcry, acting in a landscape where the natural world seems to conspire with mankind's self-brutalization. However, a quality of passionate rage transforms Goya's art, saving it from the degradation of the barbarities he portrays.

Etchings from Goya's sequence, *The Disasters of War* show mutilated and dismembered men impaled on trees. One armless and legless victim has a branch stuck up the anus. In his canvas, *The Third of May*, French soldiers are shooting terrified Spanish hostages. In such works Goya develops a new form of pictorial journalism that is also powerful art. The depictions are political and particular, provoked by the atrocities committed by French invaders in Spain, but the revulsion is cosmic and ennobling.

Artists had long looked on war with a jaundiced eye. From the fifteenth century onward Renaissance artists, including Durer, Pieter Bruegel the Elder, Mantegna, Rubens, Albrecht Altdorfer, Urs Graf and Paolo Ucello, often recorded warfare, including scenes of slaughter and suffering, that had no overtone of glory or victorious celebration. During the bloody Thirty Years War that devastated Europe in the early seventeenth century, the French artist Jacques Callot engraved a graphic series titled *The Miseries and Disasters of War*, foreshadowing Goya's etchings. But Goya was the first to make man's inhumanity to man the center of his outraged concern. He injected a new note of absolute outrage into such depictions, a vehemence that gives them tremendous emotional power. In truth, Goya's outcry is so fierce it creates its own counterforce to the atrocities he portrays.

The key to this extraordinary effect is the artist's radical stance, one that would become crucial to the whole process of making art. Goya the artist is inside his art as well as outside, a participant as well as a recorder. Goya knows that the horrors he witnesses live in his own heart, and that the artist is responsible for every aspect of his creation, no matter how terrifying. In Goya's art the screen of the canvas is ripped to shreds by the character of a world in which man is the measure of all things. The garment of art can no longer cloak the painter's soul, and he's left as naked as the next man, maybe more so.

This nakedness is revealed most brutally in Goya's "Black Paintings" series, particularly the canvas, *Saturn Devouring one of his Children*. Saturn, also known as Cronus, is a terrifying, hairy god caught in the act of tearing the headless human corpse of his son limb from limb with his bloody, gaping maw. Goya's interpretation of this ancient myth makes all men Saturnine, devourers of their own kind, and the violence Goya perceives so vividly in the human soul is only just contained within his considerable art. The feeling in his etchings and paintings is so intense, so immediate and clear-eyed, it threatens to explode the notion of art itself, mocking Immanuel Kant's cry, Dare to know! - the proud motto of the Enlightenment.

As the turbulent nineteenth century passed into the twentieth century of Auschwitz and Hiroshima, Goya's artistic struggle moved to the heart of Western culture: a battle to render the primal energies of violence degraded by a Rational Age trumpeting slogans of liberty, equality, and fraternity while descending to ever more shameful levels of primitive brutality. Many other painters have since been impelled to the same response, but they've seldom achieved Goya's potent fusion of unblinking clarity and passionate expressiveness - his absolute rapture of rage.

After Goya, Vincent van Gogh found less brutal, but no less absolute, means to express his perception of a human condition strung out between terror and yearning. Unlike Goya, however, Van Gogh's most powerful paintings marry a sense of primal fright with a rejoicing so intense we seem to hear the painter's voice singing hymns of praise to nature's annihilating generosities.

"I have a terrible lucidity at moments," [109] he wrote in 1888, two years before his death, and this brutal clarity is most evident in Van Gogh's last canvas, *Cornfield with Crows*, painted a few days before he committed suicide. The yellow corn, charged with an almost unbearable vitality, blazes with color under a dark blue sky dense as eternity. The crows that wheel over the cornfield are dots of death. In this cornfield, man in nature and nature in man crash together like particles of pure light seeking a mutual melt-down.

Van Gogh's lucid vision again shines through his 1888 canvas, *All Night Café*, which turns an ordinary tavern interior into a place where, he declared, you can be ruined, go mad and commit crimes. *All Night Café* shows a pool table surrounded by tables at which a few inebriated patrons are slumped. One can almost smell the sense of "a devil's furnace" that Van Gogh said charged the atmosphere of this low drinking den. But in the harsh light of the overhead oil lamps this small purgatory is rendered in soft greens, grainy yellow ochres and raw reds, "all with the appearance of Japanese gaiety," [110] he declared.

That juxtaposition of "devil's furnace" and "Japanese gaiety" is crucial. On the one hand, it reveals the artist's fight to contain his terrors within the formal framework of art, and no art is more formal in its strategies than the Japanese tradition. Nothing quite conveys as much sensual delight in the small moments of ordinary life than, say, a woodblock by Torii Kiyonaga showing women in a bath house, or a splendid geisha and her apprentice in an Utamaro print preparing and proffering a saucer of warm *sake*.

Yet Van Gogh's devil's furnace is utterly European in the quality of its emotional force. There's a residue there of damnation deserved, and even welcomed. Our natures consume us, *All Night Café* seems to say; and nature consumes us, says *Cornfield with Crows*. Only a violent creativity can render such a tragic sense of life; a tragic sense which yet celebrates an essential joyfulness in the annihilating glories of creation.

*L'amour est a rénventer*, Rimbaud said, and Van Gogh loved the world to death while reinventing it. His terrible lucidity links him to the anonymous Stone Age artists of Lascaux, who regarded fierce nature with a mixture of extreme fright and absolute fascination. "We can only be magicians if we are the medium of the primal forces," [111] the German architect Bruno Taut wrote, in 1919 - a declaration which rings equally true for Van Gogh and the artists of Lascaux.

Another nineteenth century magician of the primal forces was the English painter, William Turner. Turner's 1842 canvas of a snow storm at sea is an elemental vortex in which tumultuous, swirling yellow pigments obliterate the lines between sky and water. A fiery red whirlwind is an arrow of fury, a shaft aimed at a black ship that is hardly more than a smudge on the obliterated horizon. Nature's tumult swallows all light, sucks all life down into a ferocity that threatens both annihilation and salvation.

To experience the immediacy of such a tempest, Turner had himself lashed to the mast of ship. The storm was Turner's Moby-Dick, and in his pursuit of its power the painter was Captain Ahab chasing the white whale, hounding a splendid creature that could kill him. Turner, like all such would-be sorcerers, yearned to capture creation's potency and wild style, knowing all the while that nature is too vivid to imitate in all its force and glory. It can only be magically rendered in brilliant flashes, in the blink of an eye glimpsing the sun, or in a stolen glance.

The complex human tug between apprehension and ecstasy in the face of nature was noted by Leonardo da Vinci. He spoke of "the man who with perpetual longing always looks forward with joy to each new spring and each new summer...and who does not perceive that he is longing for his own destruction." This longing is an elemental spirit, Leonardo wrote; a spirit which, "finding itself imprisoned in the human body, desires continually to return to its source." [112] Andre Malraux expressed it more bluntly: "Nietzsche has written that when we see a meadow ablaze with the flowers of spring, the thought that the whole human race is no more than a luxuriant growth of the same order, created to no end by some blind force, would be unbearable, could we bring ourselves to realize all that the thought implies." [113] In a 1918 credo, the artist Max Beckmann declared: "I try to capture the terrible, thrilling monster of life's vitality and to confine it, to beat it down and strangle it with crystal-clear, razor-sharp lines and planes." [114]

Franz Kafka composed an ironic aphorism about crows, that Van Gogh would have appreciated. "Crows claim that a single crow could destroy heaven. Doubtless that is so, but it proves nothing against heaven; heaven simply signifies: the impossibility of crows." [115]

The barbarity Goya rendered was wholly destructive, but there are other kinds of barbarity, those that invigorate an exhausted and corrupted culture. Gide's appeal for barbarians to revive the flagging energies of European art was enthusiastically taken up by artists at the turn of the century.

"Throw yourself into whiteness with me, fellow pilots, and swim into infinity," the Russian Suprematist painter Kasimir Malevich exhorted. "I have trampled the frontiers of colored skies underfoot, uprooted them, made them into a sack into which I have thrown all colors." [116] In Italy, the Futurist artist Filippo Tommaso Marinetti cried that modern man was "in at the birth of the centaurs, we shall see the angels fly. We must rattle the doors of life, test the hinges and the bolts." [117]

Impelled by the same mood of vibrant iconoclasm, Pablo Picasso created his shattering 1907 canvas, *Les Demoiselles d'Avignon,* in which a bunch of Barcelona whores display a barbaric eroticism that disintegrates their bodies into a jagged geometry. *Les Demoiselles* was provocative in the violence of its manner; a manner which, in its willful fragmentation, demolished the conventions of the European art canons that went back to Giotto and the early fourteenth century. Picasso's vision splintered old European concepts of reality, embodied in such artistic conventions as perspective and the single point of view it implies. Suddenly, things could be seen from many sides at once, to become known in their essence rather than their surfaces. Picasso's art epitomizes twentieth-century artistic endeavor, described by a contemporary critic as "man's rage for chaos... the reinforcement of the capacity to endure disorientation so that a real and significant problem may emerge." [118]

Chaos runs riot in George Grosz's raging 1917 canvases *Me-*

*tropolis and Explosion.* Fiery reds, shattered by urban violence into fragments one might see through a windowpane cracked by flames, light up a world gone mad with war and revolution. Otto Dix and Kathe Kollwitz depict the disasters of World War One, the conflict that is the suicide of Old Europe; the self-immolation of that man of the Enlightenment Jean-Jacques Rousseau once bravely declared was born free.

In a series of hand-colored woodcuts, Otto Lange shows us a suicidal Christ in his ultimate agony, suffering a self-inflicted Passion of jagged, blood-red wounds. Max Beckmann's set of prints, titled simply *Hell,* illustrate the antechambers of a limbo filled with Europe's tortured victims and leering tormentors.

Chaotic rage is also a favored Surrealist strategy. Visitors to Surrealism's show at Cologne in 1920 are handed axes and urged to destroy the exhibits. In Max Ernst's ironic canvas, *The Angel of Hearth and Home,* the angel is a ravening demon bursting from a tree in the act of transforming itself into a creature with a beak and fangs. In *Europe After the Rain* Ernst conjures up a post-nuclear landscape of ruined, half-melted forms that presages Hiroshima. This painting is completed in 1942, three years before the bomb is dropped, and well before it is even known to be a technological possibility.

Clearly, the modern rage for chaos is all about us. It's evident in the violent street art of graffiti that decorates urban walls, buses and subway cars; in the self-mutilating performance artists who slash their wrists and bleed onto canvases or poke skewers through their cheeks; in the graphic messages about the scourge of AIDS that has particularly devastated the creative community.

Man's rage against himself has become a major theme of the visual arts, fueled by the growing gap between rapid technological advance and social regression, between a rampant materialism and a deepening hunger for "meaning." The belief that art is a creative force that can transform every human or natural event no longer holds sway. Today, artists appear capable only of enduring, deploring, or struggling to cope with naked terror - a terror uncoupled from rapture.

# 4
# violence made visible

Seen from below, the hilltop palace of the Alhambra in Granada resembles a geode, one of those rocks whose skin is rough and plain but whose innards are a trove of brilliant crystals. This sharp contrast between a simple, rugged surface and an intricate, glowing core is the Alhambra's profound appeal, derived from a dynamic tension between craggy battlements and the fragile Moorish pavilions sheltered within. In effect, the Red Citadel's architecture's transforms the threat of violent attack into a superb visual metaphor, charged with a particular poignancy and a powerful compositional intensity.

Each time you approach the Alhambra from the city below you relive this experience of a vividly expressive form generated by the pressure of violence. Walking up the long, steep road toward the Alhambra, you watch the low evening sun set fire to the snowy peaks of the Sierra Nevada while shadows turn the red sandstone walls of the Moorish palace the color of dried blood. The urban uproar of the city of Granada falls away below as you ascend through the avenue of elms, planted by the Duke of Wellington in his campaign against Napoleon's occupying army. The elms share the sky with noble chestnuts, their white candles aflame in the spring air, and you may fancy you hear the dusk song of the English nightingales the Duke is said to have set free among the trees.

Approaching the Gate of Justice, you come face to face with the connection between a stark defensive exterior and the inward serenity this architectural armor makes possible. Beyond the gate, skirting the pompous Renaissance palace built by the Christian Emperor Charles the Fifth, you slip through a side entrance into the Court of the Myrtles. This quiet pavilion, with its wide reflecting pool mirroring delicate colonnades, offers the first taste of the Alhambra's rich interior life. There's a reminder here of the robust protective exterior in the blunt mass of the crenellated Comares Tower looming overhead, its solid bulk superimposed upon the suppleness of the court's arcades. This court, like every enclosure in the Red Citadel, is charged with metaphoric meaning suggesting the meeting of landscape and sky, the link between heaven and earth, the striking opposition of outer turbulence and inner tranquility.

Searching about, you find the narrow door that leads into the neighboring Court of the Lions, the heart of the Alhambra. But the path is not easy; the whole palace resembles a labyrinth in which seemingly obvious portals may be dead ends and hidden narrow side openings lead in the right direction. In this, the Alhambra recalls the fabled City of Brass in *The 1001 Nights*, where secret passageways and tiny doorways are the true openings between one glimpse of paradise and another. In both instances, if you're not an initiate into the mysteries of the place, you'll fumble to find the right pathway.

Though it takes three offset doorways to get there, you finally enter the Court of the Lions. The act of entry makes your pulse beat faster; you need a moment to adjust your mind to the quantum leap in complexity and subtlety its architecture offers.

The court is small, only 93'6" by 51'6", but everything the Alhambra intends is manifest here, at the peak of its expression. The dancing, lightfooted colonnades - an irregular rhythm of twinned and single pillars slender as reeds - support lacy stucco porticoes. In the column capitals the Arabic calligraphy that decorates the walls evolves into pure, foliated ornament, which in turn rises into elaborately patterned geometries. This glory of inscribed meaning celebrates the great Nasrid king Muhammad the Fifth - he who was "rich in God" - who commissioned this court. "How many joyful solaces for the eyes are to be found in it," wrote the fourteenth century court poet, Ibn Zamrak. "Here even the dreamer will renew the objects of his desire!" [119]

In the center of the court is the lion fountain, supported by a dozen beasts, like the gilded throne King Solomon created for the Queen of Sheba when she visited him in Jerusalem. The lion fountain sits on a crux of water runnels that link the court with its four surrounding halls, much as paradise was supposed to be the source of four rivers.

The geode metaphor applies most dramatically to the Hall of the Two Sisters, one of the Court of Lion's side chambers. Within its crude external mass is a golden honeycomb of stucco stalactites known as *muquarnas*, creating the sensation of an infinitely faceted heavenly dome rotating with the sun, moon and stars. Seen at sunset, the dome's honeyed light conjures up the Palanquin of Solomon, which, in poet Ibn Gabirol's phrase, "rotates on its gyre, shining like opals and sapphires and pearls." [120]

In this remarkable small space, architecture as structure and as symbol seamlessly fuse. Colonnades, ceilings, water, inscriptions poetic and holy meld magically into a floating world lifted high above the city into a symphonic realm dense with meaning. Architecture, like music, has a direct path to the spirit. There is no more basic human expression than the shaping of shelter, unless it is the need for song, and this architecture sings to the soul. "Contemplate my beauty and you will be penetrated with understanding," goes a line from the Ibn Zamrak poem, expressing the afterglow any visitor carries away from the Arab Al-hamra.

*   *   *

On the face if it, it may seem that architecture is the last place to look for any manifestation of violence as a creative force. More concretely than any other activity, architecture symbolizes mankind's pursuit of ordered social structures, and there are few sights more disturbing than a house, town, or city shattered by bombs or flattened by floods or hurricanes.

Over the millennia, however, both the actuality and the threat of turbulence have shaped human shelter at least as much as any other factor. Architecture has been described as society made visible, and it follows that the character of human settlement has been greatly influenced by the urgent need to respond to the prevalence of violence in the world at large. "Man is in a kind of cyclone," Le Corbusier wrote in *When the Cathedrals Were White.* "He builds solid houses to protect and shelter his heart. Outside, nature is nothing but indifference, even terror." [121]

Many of our towns and buildings would look very different if such terror, whether natural or manmade, were not such a potent factor in shaping the history of human habitation. Indeed, some of our most eloquent acts of architecture would not exist without the urgent need to respond creatively to both the reality and the threat of violence, and one may characterize much of what mankind has built over the millennia as violence made visible.

From the beginning, people have found imaginative ways to contrive buildings and settlements that simultaneously counter and implicitly integrate the reality of violence as a shaping force. They have fortified their towns, made bastions of their castles, walled their palaces and ringed their holy places with protective towers. Throughout the history of construction, resourceful responses to threat have given form to dwellings, streets, cities, palaces and sanctuaries in both direct and subtle ways. This tonic sense of danger has spurred people to invent the kind of architecture that not only defends and protects, but also transforms the impact of violence into moving symbols of shelter.

In the Neolithic era men built Ggantija, the "Tower of the Giants," on the Maltese island of Gozo. Ggantija's thick limestone walls guarded a labyrinth of temples, creating a womb-like security that harked back to the protection provided by cave dwellings, such as those at Lascaux and Altamira. Also in the period we call prehistory, men erected the Sardinian nuraghi, tall cones put together out of piled stones for safety against predators, both human and animal, in a harsh landscape. Later came the similarly constructed southern Italian trulli and the Scottish stone citadels called brochs. In the United States, between 1100 and 1300 AD, the Anasazi peoples of the Southwest constructed the defensive settlement known as Pueblo Bonito in New Mexico's Chaco Canyon, and the dramatic cliff villages of Colorado's Mesa Verde.

Shelters were devised not only for the living. The bodies and spirits of the dead were guarded by massive tombs designed to keep desecrators and demons at bay. Structures created for the burial of ancestors and the worship of their spirits reveal one of the deepest impulses in the human psyche: the need to honor or appease the ghosts of the departed, which were believed capable of the most frightful retribution if not given their due.

The Pyramids and the rock-cut tombs of the Valley of the Kings of Ancient Egypt were designed to guard mummified royalty and its worldly artifacts from violation. In a culture that gave a more lasting significance to the hereafter than the here-and-now, the Nile Pyramids were eternal castles enclosing the burial chambers in which a person's *ka*, his emanation of the universal life force, might forever survive the turbulence of the temporal world. Other examples of fortress graves, such as the Tomb of Agamemnon at Mycenae, though less grand than the Pyramids, had the same intention to secure the sanctity of the bones and the spirits of the deceased against attack.

The millennia before the birth of Christ witnessed the construction of Biblical Jericho and Ur, India's Mohenjo-Daro, the fabled fortress city of Ubar in Oman, and Hellenic Troy, Argos and Thebes - all magnificently walled. The 2,000-mile-long Great Wall of China, built to hold barbarian hordes at bay, is history's most ambitious act of architectural engineering. Christians created a fortified Constantinople while Muslims built Tunisia's Kairawan, Spain's Granada, Morocco's Marrakesh, and Ottoman Jerusalem. The Incas erected Cuzco's Sacsahuaman fortress, Africans the citadel of Zimbabwe in southern Africa. In the troubled European middle ages many superb walled cities were built, including Paris, Dubrovnik, Carcasonne, Toledo and Avila.

The camps of the Vikings, who terrorized Christian and Muslim territories from the ninth century on, were pure defensive circles protected by double walls with small gates at each quarter. Viking camps, such as Trelleborg, Denmark, were further divided within their segments into square compounds that could be separately defended against assault by sea or land. The circular and square shapes seen in Trelleborg were emblematic forms common to many defensive structures; they reflected an instinctively Platonic order and simplicity set against the chaos and uncertainty of the larger world.

In response to raiders and pirates such as the Vikings, many Mediterranean towns and villages took to the hilltops. Here again the defensive reflex shaped a distinctive and appealing architecture. Tuscan towns such as Pitigliano, Castelnuovo and San Gimignano, Southern Italian towns such as Ostuni, and the Peleponnesian village of Vatheia responded to the twin threat of human marauders and lowland malarial mosquitoes. The iconic form of these hilltop habitations, which seem to spring from the topography like natural growths, are among the purest expressions of architecture as violence made visible.

Buildings, towns and cities molded by the pressures of violence display a distinctive simplicity and compression. It is as if the forces pressing in upon them have compacted their silhouettes and stripped away the elaborations indulged in by more expansive architectures. Their outlines can often be read at a glance, providing a kind of capsule commentary on the human presence in a natural and social landscape always haunted by some kind of danger. Tuscan hilltop towns, Suleiman the Magnificent's Jerusalem, Granada's Alhambra and such walled cities as Avila and Carcasonne are acts of visual concentration, vibrant with allusion. At a glance, these places tell quick stories about the way people have transformed the pressure of violence into vivid enclaves.

*    *    *

The wall-busting long-range cannon forcibly changed the con-figuration of European towns from the fifteenth century onward. The growth of trade in the late Middle Ages, and the rise of the property-owning middle class, caused many city walls to come tum-bling down. As towns spread out into the open countryside, inter-nal criminal activity rather than any external military threat became a prime shaper of urban form.

In reaction to this, towns were divided into defensive precincts. Whereas in the medieval urban warren all classes under the lord or seigneur lived jumbled together, post-medieval towns moved to-ward a separation into class-bound districts, to protect the haves from the often ferocious envy of the have-nots.

Streets and houses became private realms seeking protection against the public arena. Residences were either grouped around private squares, such as those in London's Kensington and Belgravia, or were guarded by gates, as in the Parisian private *hotel particulaire* and the Venetian palazzo. Or they were hidden behind blank walls, as in Seville and Marrakesh. The concept of "security," in the mod-ern sense of protection from criminals out for rape, theft and even murder, began to govern the design of buildings and streets within the city limits.

This sense of an internalized threat provoked the eighteenth century engraver Giovanni Battista Piranesi to charge his prints with renderings of Rome in the grip of an imagined decay. Piranesi attacked the Renaissance's fond belief in an eternal Classical order, and opened the door to creative chaos. The visual violence of his *Carceri*, a series of etchings depicting imaginary prison interiors, dissolves space into light in a meltdown of solid shapes. This ruined, illusionary architecture presaged Einstein's concept that visible mass and invisible energy are essentially interchangeable phenomena.

Piranesi's violated structures hum with the pathos of decadence, releasing meanings hidden by ordered architectures. The sense of imminent collapse that haunts their halls hints at the slow-motion assault of time and the elements upon the work of man. In their evocations of collapse, Piranesi's etchings provide the same kind of ambiguous pleasure provoked by the contemplation of architectural ruins, which add the dimension of entropy to the act of building, and touch hidden nerves of insecurity most structures implicitly strive to suppress.

In this vein, the eighteenth-century English architect John Vanbrugh urged the Duchess of Marlborough to preserve the derelict old manor house in the grounds of her splendid new Blenheim Palace, to remind herself that all glory passes and every act of creation is threatened by destruction. Vanbrugh's sentiments implied that every building is to some extent a defiance of nature; a defiance that must ultimately fail, no matter how grandiose its ambitions. Shelley expressed this vividly in *Ozymandias*, speaking of the shattered statue of the grandiose "king of kings," he wrote: "Round the decay/ Of that colossal wreck, boundless and bare/ The lone and level sands stretch far away." [122]

Looked at more romantically, ruins can remind us of vanished glories, of civilizations we imagine may have been more gracious than our own. But they also appeal to our appetite for a kind of creative destruction, a dark desire for the apocalyptic.

Writer Rebecca West put it this way: "Only part of us is sane. Only part of us loves pleasure and the longer day of happiness, wants to live to our nineties and die in peace, in a house that we built, that shall shelter those who come after us. The other half of us is nearly mad. It prefers the disagreeable to the agreeable, loves pain and its darker night despair, and wants to die in a catastrophe that will set life back to its beginnings and leave nothing of our house save its blackened foundations." [123]

* * *

There is another sense in which architectural creativity has been stimulated by the energies of violence. The reactive response to turbulence and threat, that has given form to so much of our architecture, has at times been matched by a proactive urge to generate structures that look as if a furious nature itself were the designer. Temples that resemble frozen eruptions burst forth in the landscape of India and Cambodia between the eleventh and thirteenth centuries. Indian temples at Khajuraho, Konarak and Somnathpur appear to be volcanic upthrusts of raw rock. Erotic figures in hectic acts of lust and passion agitate the walls of Khajuraho, to celebrate a divine Creation that is also charged with fleshly appetites. The Indian temples, like those at Angkor Wat and Angkor Thom in Cambodia, are covered with carvings so vigorous they make the stone come vehemently alive. With their horizontal striations and vertical pleating, these structures directly mimic the tumult of geological forces.

William Temple, an early eighteenth century English traveler, reported the presence in the Chinese landscape of "broken, crumbling contorted rocks with numerous outcroppings" carved into sculptures which exuberantly exaggerated the geological forces that created them. The Mandarin Chinese term for such phenomena is *sa-ro-(k) wai-chi*, (translated as "disordered grace" a term Temple transmuted into "Sharawadgi" or "Sharawaggi." Exercising an unusual receptivity for a man of his time and culture, Temple observed that "The Chinese devote their entire minds, which are extremely inventive, to imagining shapes that will be of great beauty and that will astonish the eye, but which will not be redolent of the order and arrangement that immediately attracts the attention." [124]

A moving mimicry of violent nature characterized the designs of Antonio Gaudi. Working in Barcelona at the turn of the century, Gaudi designed a series of spaces and buildings, from parks and apartment houses to the famed Church of the Holy Family: a composition of volcanic towers that challenge heaven while melting like hot lava. In the crypt of the unfinished Chapel of the Colonia Guell in the Catalonian countryside, Gaudi conjured an extraordinary space of canted, rough-hewn stone columns supporting a spray of brick arches that appear to be in eruption. Lantern windows of stained glass, shaped like huge, polychromatic daisies, fill the interior with a lurid light, giving the crypt the feeling of the catacombs in which Roman Christianity first took secret root.

The Colonia Guell crypt is a display of elemental building technologies, a radical act of rudimentary architecture by a sophisticated talent acting as a true magician of the primal forces. In the words of an architectural historian, "the crypt's concept is both severe and serene, expressed through a voluntary and ascetic primitivism, which moves from harshness to violence, to produce the paradox of a destructive construction." [125]

The paradox of destructive construction that gives Gaudi's architecture its energy galvanized a host of radical designers in the early years of the twentieth century. Eager to smash the mold of an increasingly sterile vocabulary of styles, they declared, in the words of visionary architect Antonio Sant'Elia, that "Architecture, exhausted by tradition, begins again, forcibly from the beginning." [126]

Suprematists and Constructivists in Russia, Futurists in Italy, and the Crystal Chain group in Germany were moved by a passionate urge to clear the decks. "Get hold of picks, axes, hammers and demolish, demolish without pity the venerable cities," [127] the Futurists trumpeted. In his 1914 *Citta Nuova*, Sant'Elia demanded a modern city characterized by "raw, naked and violently colored materials." [128] In Germany, architect Hans Scharoun, declared that "Passionate forces, freed from the central focus of the red dawn of mankind, are moving in rhythm. If they are weak, they hardly break away from the core. When they are strong, however, they fill the conceptual voids with a maelstrom of passionate fantasy." [129]

In post-Tsarist Russia, Suprematist El Lissitzky and Constructivist Vladimir Tatlin dreamed up imaginary architectures for a visionary future of social justice. Tatlin's 1920 project for a Monument and Headquarters of the Third Communist International in Moscow was an icon of revolution. Intended to be 1,000 feet high, taller than the Eiffel Tower, the Monument featured a pair of angled, interlaced lattice spirals painted bright red. The spirals enclosed three suspended volumes - a cube, a pyramid and a cylinder - containing state congress halls designed to rotate at different speeds to mark the year, month and day. The model, carpented together out of cigar-box wood and tin cans, drew enthusiastic crowds.

Off-balance structures entranced the Russian avant-garde. El Lissitzky's 1920 design for Lenin's Tribune looked as if it had been knocked off the vertical by some powerful gale. Alexander Rodchenko's 1920 sketch for a Party radio station seemed to have been disassembled by a seismic eruption into a jumble of masts, guy wires and floating fragments. Nikolai Ladovsky's 1920 project for a communal house was a distorted warren, a wild, cantilevered, eccentric construction with a skeletal steel arm shooting out into space.

Such built-in imbalance reflected a world in which old structures were toppling, clearing the decks for a fresh invention. "I exhausted myself in the summoning roar of Nature (coming to me) from somewhere remote and profound, as if through a sort of thicket," [130] wrote architect Konstantin Melnikov. Though most of these projects and declarations remained in the realm of sketches and rhetoric rather than actual architecture, they expressed a deep desire for a radical renewal and an urge to give form to feelings seldom associated with architecture.

Architecture critic Bruno Zevi, referring to the designs created by the German expressionist architect Erich Mendelsohn, vehemently refuted the notion that buildings are incapable of rendering extreme emotions. "It is generally considered that architecture cannot express states of feeling, such as love, fear, sadness, disgust, enthusiasm or despair," he wrote. But Mendelsohn's eloquent designs and drawings are filled with swirling forms representing, "A cry, chaos and geometry... [in] a tempestuous space." [131]

Half a century later, an urge for chaotic geometries found fresh expression in a mannerism dubbed "Deconstructivism." First manifested in the 1970s, Deconstructivism was formally canonized as a movement in its own right in the 1988 show at New York's Museum of Modern Art. Deconstructivism is "an aesthetic of danger," MoMA's catalog declared, featuring "unstable, reckless... forms exploded from within." [132]

The new architecture of deconstruction sprang from a growing frustration with the rigid form-follows-function ideology of the Modernist movement which dominated world architecture in the decades following World War Two. At the same time, designers began to take account of the visually chaotic character of many modern cities, where so many structures seem makeshift, tacky, and downright ugly, yet remain vigorously populist in their appeal.

A decade before Deconstructivism was given a formal tag, several innovative designers were already subjecting their buildings to torture. The New York-based design group, SITE Projects, created a series of startling showrooms for the Best Products Company of Richmond, Virginia, a national chain of general merchandise stores. The first SITE-designed Best store was the 1972 "Peeling Wall" showroom in Richmond, Virginia, in which a standard suburban shopping center structure was given a front facade that looked as if it were about to fall away from the rest of the building.

SITE followed the "Peeling Wall" with a series of architectural deconstructions of Best stores in Houston, Texas, Sacramento, California and Towson, Maryland. Most striking of them all was the "Indeterminate Facade," in the Alameda-Genoa shopping center in a suburb of Houston. The front and side white brick walls of this building seem to be crumbling away in a state of imminent collapse - a veritable ruin in progress. A massive pile of bricks heaped upon the front canopy suggests the unrest lurking beneath the bland surface of suburban comfort and convenience.

SITE principal James Wines calls his firm's style "De-architecture." He speaks about "the fascination of missing parts" in architecture. "In our age, when the monolithic structures are crumbling under their own weight, it is really `missing parts' and fragmentary pieces that represent the real vitality of urban life." [133]

A professional critic said that "SITE's juxtaposition of the modestly familiar with the stunningly unfamiliar is like a bomb that arrives in a shoebox." [134] But the reaction of the local populace to Houston's 1975 "Indeterminate Facade" was wildly enthusiastic. "That's just what I've always wanted to do - kick the shit out of one of those buildings," one citizen commented. [135] In the years after its opening, the Houston store exceeded expected sales records by a whopping forty percent, proving Best Products' commercial shrewdness in commissioning such radical designs.

In its Best showroom series, SITE engendered a truly American event: an architecture that, like comic books and cartoons, speaks to the anarchic, populist, kick-over-the-traces impulse that continually disrupts and invigorates American culture. Here the formal esthetic of "high" architecture is flipped over to reveal the crude, vigorous "low" architecture of its underside, releasing a tonic creative energy.

Frank Gehry - another, and much more influential, American iconoclast - emerged in Southern California in the late 1970s. Less articulate but more intuitive than Wines, Gehry cracked the shell of Modernism with a violent vernacular of his own.

Gehry's first experiment in this drastic mannerism was inflicted upon his own house, in Santa Monica. Gehry took a modest suburban box, clad in salmon-pink-painted asbestos shingles, and transformed it by an act of creative destruction. Tearing away the old shingles, he exposed the skeleton of the original stud framing, then added new screen walls of corrugated metal and chain link fencing in a deliberate distortion. The sense of dislocation is enhanced by the skewed, cubical bay window/skylight over the kitchen area, which appears to have been dropped off the back of a truck by clumsy handlers. Under this attack a conventional house is disrupted and reordered. Suburban tranquility is rudely invaded by the realities of the surrounding city, by the rough, fragmented presence of a Los Angeles Gehry describes as "bits and pieces of industrial buildings and freeways." [136]

Most of Gehry's buildings are exploded and reassembled to reveal new meanings of order and form. "What I like best is breaking down the project into as many separate parts as possible," he said, to free multiple images that "can relate to all kinds of symbolic things, ideas that you've liked, places you've liked, bits and pieces of your life that you would like to recall." He added: "I like playing at the edge of disaster." [137]

Playing at the edge of disaster, American architect Daniel Liebeskind designed a new Jewish Museum in Berlin to commemorate the historic and troubled relationship between Germany and the Jews as a dance of cacophonic, symbolic geometries. Configured like a zigzag lightning bolt, the dread insignia of the Nazi SS, or variously a distorted Star of David, the plan conjures up memories of violence and destruction, and suggests a new kind of architecture emerging from the ashes of World War Two and the often brutal Cold War that followed. What is remarkable about this building as an act of architecture is its ambition to integrate a graphic metaphor of violence within the actual fabric of the structure. In this sense it harks back to the "disordered grace" of those sculpted Chinese rock formations William Temple described.

Jagged shapes of glass and steel jut out at all angles in the 1988 remodeling of the rooftop attic of a Beaux-Arts style apartment building in Vienna's Falkestrasse. As contrived by the Austrian design group Coop Himmelblau, or Blue Sky Cooperative, the Falkestrasse attic underwent an architectural Caesarian, the surgical eruption of a creature out of its own innards.

This creature is "a writhing disruptive animal breaking through the corner," the architects declared, a "skeletal monster which breaks up the elements of form as it struggles out...(as) the roof splits, shears and buckles." [138] This description, which recalls a startling scene in the movie *Alien*, signaled a vitality bursting through the smug Biedermeier facades of post-Nazi Vienna. Coop Himmelblau's alien intrusion forced new emotional and visual meanings from the old building. Tortured from within by an attacking style its designers describe as "bleeding," by an "architecture that lights up, that stings, that rips, and under stress, tears," [139] the conservative structure confesses the "crime" of its false and dangerous complacency.

A similar, if more subtle disruption of traditional form is found in the work of the American architect Peter Eisenman. In some of his projects, such as his 1970 "House III," in Lakeville, Connecticut, conflicting grids of planes and piers are rotated diagonally at 45 degrees to one another to set up "angular collisions throughout the house which are dramatic and even violent." [140] The structure of this small house seems to spin around its internal spaces, unbalanced at every angle, like an unsolved Rubik's Cube. "Architectural enjoyment consists...in this game of mentally manipulating relationships, inverting and rotating them." [141]

\*   \*   \*

The "creative destruction" of the structures cited above shines a harsh light on the profound ambiguities that have crippled modern architecture from its beginnings in the late nineteenth century. Under its often trumpeted ambition to make the world a better place by making better buildings, Modernism has all too often failed to voice the guilty knowledge that in practice it has mostly served aggressive social or economic masters unencumbered by such highminded aspirations.

This uneasy disjunction between ambition and reality surfaced in early arguments over that prime icon of urban modernity, the skyscraper; a building that is simultaneously a negative, deeply antiurban response to the insecurity of modern city streets and a supreme act of mercantile smugness. Skyscrapers - the name itself is aggressive - turn communal thoroughfares into a deep canyons of danger and distrust, complacent in the blunt expression of economic power their skyward thrust embodies. This architectural arrogance is most evident when these glittering towers are viewed from the desolate sidewalks of the lowdown skid rows that surround most American downtowns.

At the birth of the skyscraper form in Chicago in the 1880s and '90s, architect Louis Sullivan, one of the godfathers of the highrise style, fretted over its inherent social and aesthetic barbarism. He asked: "How shall we impart to this sterile pile, this crude, harsh, brutal agglomeration, this stark exclamation of eternal strife, the graciousness of the higher forms of sensibility and culture that rest on the lower and fiercer passions." [142] Sullivan's answer was to imbue the new skyscraper with "the force and power of altitude," [143] but very few tall modern office buildings have achieved the graciousness he sought. New York City's Chrysler Building and Seagram Building, and Norman Foster's Hong Kong and Shanghai Banking Corporation building in Hong Kong are among the rare exceptions; yet even these fine structures cannot escape the shadow of Sullivan's "sterile pile" and "brutal agglomeration." And all three share in the negative impact of the skyscraper on the urban environment.

In the skyscraper, architecture is violence made visible, but without the transformation that turns a fortress like the Alhambra into a sublime symbol. Maybe the commercial highrise, like the airport terminal, is too blunt a revelation of the crude imperatives that drive so much of modern life to lend itself to any civilized metamorphosis. In truth, contemporary commercial culture has become so charged with veiled economic violence at every level of its operation - a violence simultaneously abstract and internalized, inseparable from its sinews yet difficult to pin down - that its vigor can seldom be transmuted into any kind of visual imagery other than that of sleek power.

This leads one to ponder the difference between architectures that can transform violence and the threat of violence into supreme metaphors, and those that fail to do so. Is it because, in the case of the skyscraper, those instincts of transformation, Sullivan's "higher forms of sensibility," are entirely absent? And does that absence spring from our fundamental lack of cultural, as against purely commercial, confidence?

Perhaps we should seek an answer to these vital questions at a larger scale than the individual building or complex - in the radical evolution of the postmodern metropolis in the late twentieth century. Cities such as Paris, London, Tokyo, Sao Paulo, Mexico City, New York and Los Angeles are now vast regional conglomerations with populations in the many millions. These major economic power centres trade with one another, leaping local and even national boundaries in a hard-charging global economy that owes no loyalty to cultural traditions or aspirations.

"In the 1980s the industrial city finally shook off the last traces of its 19th century self and mutated into a completely new species," Deyan Sudjic declares in *The 100 Mile City*. "Migration and economic development changed it beyond recognition. Technological innovations eliminated traditional industries and scattered new ones in unpredictable places over ever wider distances." [144]

Searching for a metaphor to describe this new urban phenomenon, Sudjic writes: "Imagine the force field around a high tension power line, crackling with energy and ready to discharge 20,000 volts at any point along its length, and you have some idea of the modern city as it enters the last decade of the century." [145] He continues: "To accept this image of the city is to accept uncomfortable things about ourselves, and our illusions about the way we want to live. The city is as much about selfishness and fear as it is about community and civic life. And yet to accept that the city has a dark side, of menace and greed, does not diminish its vitality and strength. In the last analysis, it reflects man and all his potential."

The Dutch architect Rem Koolhaas puts it this way: "If there is to be a new urbanism it will not be based on the twin fantasies of order and omnipotence; it will be a staging of uncertainty... it will no longer aim for stable configurations, but for the creation of enabling fields that accommodate processes that refuse to be crystallized into definitive form... it will be obsessed with ... the reinvention of psychological space." [146] - a space that best serves the capricious global economy with its constant technological advances and need for rapid market response.

We can only hope that, once the new metropolitan phenomenon stabilizes, this volatile "staging of uncertainty" will generate cultural initiatives that create their own transfigurations of the crude energies charging its nature; that architecture will once again demonstrate its ancient power to metamorphose violent forces into moving images of transformation.

For good or ill, there can be no doubt of the prime role violence has played in giving form to architecture. One way or another, violence has shaped architecture around the globe from the beginning of building, whether as a reactive response to physical or metaphysical threat, as a positive desire to imitate the potent creativity of the natural world, as a blunt revelation of crude economic and social forces, or as an attempt to reflect the emotional tenor of a troubled society.

Without the need to react to the threat of attack there would be no architectural masterpieces such as the Alhambra, no Mesa Verdes or walled Jerusalems, no Toledos or fortified palaces. Joshua's priests would never have blown down the walls of Jericho with blasts of rams' horns and a great shout; the seige of Troy would never have given us the *Iliad.* And without the esthetic upheavals of the twentieth century our architecture might still be frozen in a barren premodern mimicry of traditional mannerisms.

Creative responses to violence have shaped the built environment in more ways that we recognize. Such responses have been a power for innovation, renewal and refreshment, an original energy charging human structures, a turbulence transformed. Without it our man-made context would be much less expressive of the uniquely human capacity to transmute the forces of violence into images of glory.

# 5
# righteous wars, creative conquests & justified rebellions

War is the most dramatic and the most terrible of all forms of human violence. For most soldiers and civilians caught up in its furies, war is hell. How, then, can war's turbulence be considered creative? How can armed conflict become, in Yeats's resonant phrase, a terrible beauty in whose wake belief will be changed and civilization renewed?

The answer is complex, but in the end it boils down to two factors. The first is that war, as Lenin remarked, is the great accelerator of events, history at high speed, frequently spurring rapid cultural, social, economic and technological shifts that might otherwise have taken generations to effect. The second factor is that, historically, conquests have often created cultural cross-fertilizations which have greatly enhanced both the conquered peoples and their conquerors.

The ways in which military conquest has advanced the cross-fertilization of cultures have been noted alike by anthropologists and historians. In a truly creative conquest, the cultural character of the conquerors is enriched by absorbing the qualities of the vanquished. After the victor's aura of dominance dissipates, the mingled culture emerges as a new form, a hybrid civilization that often transcends the genius of its separate sources.

"When a warlike, aggressive, nomadic population occupies the territory of sedentary agricultural tribes, we often find that the emergent commonwealth possesses a much higher type of culture than either of its component parts," [147] noted cultural anthropologist Bronislaw Malinowski. War always remains cruel and bloody, Malinowski cautioned, but it is also a positive factor in human advance. "We can say that a war which in its results produces through conquest, federation, or amalgamation a wider cultural framework may play a constructive part in human evolution." [148] Such conflicts can, in Malinowski's view, culminate in "the harnessing of aggression by culture." [149] Malinowski also noted that military strife can have a tonic effect within the society of each warring antagonist. "We must emphasize that when war functions creatively, the centralized political organization resumes once more its positive role as protector of the people." [150]

Going even further, the military historian John Keegan suggests that the more complex war and weaponry become, the more they spur human development. "Had stone, bronze and the horse remained the means by which war was fought, its scope and intensity might never have exceeded the levels experienced during the first millennium BC," he writes, adding that, as a consequence, societies "might never have evolved far beyond pastoralism and animal husbandry." [151] Quoting anthropologist H. Turney-High, Keegan states that cultures had to rise above the basic "military horizon" if they were to move beyond the pre-state level we consider primitive.

To achieve an evolved condition of statehood, societies had to wage organized warfare, encouraging "the rise of the army with officers." [152] The evolution of the Roman army, Keegan asserts, exactly served Roman civilization itself; Rome's laws and physical infrastructure were derived from its army, and Roman military engineers built most of the roads, bridges and aqueducts that were the sinews of its social and cultural cohesion. "History lessons remind us that the states in which we live, their institutions, even their laws, have come to us through conflict, often of the most bloodthirsty sort." [153]

Where complex civilizations first appeared, in the rich alluvial valleys of the Ganges, the Euphrates, the Yellow River and the Nile, in the jungles of Central America and the mountain ranges of the Andes, warfare leading to constructive conquest made its evolutionary mark. Conquerors out of the steppes of Central Asia, from the deserts of North Africa, from the forests of Mexico and Gautemala and the peaks of Peru brought a political discipline and advanced social organization to the farmers, craftsmen and artists of the agricultural lowlands they overran and occupied. Like Moses's Children of Israel, they carried elaborate codes of law, backed by covenant, ceremony and coercion. When the nomadic, aggressive Hebrews conquered the peaceful Canaanite farmers, they laid the foundation for a rich cultural synthesis whose reverberations are still felt today.

In the millennia before the Roman Empire dominated the Western world, there was a long history of major creative conquests around the Mediterranean. Early on came the Akkadian infiltration and overthrow of Sumeria in the twenty-fourth century BC. Sargon, the first Akkadian monarch, created a regime that united the often contentious Sumerian cities into a stable state that covered northern Mesopotamia, and the Akkadians absorbed Sumerian art, architecture and literature. After the Akkadian Empire collapsed two centuries later, a revived Sumerian state erected the fabulous ziggurat in the city of Ur, where biblical Abraham was born.

In another prime instance of a fruitful, pre-Roman invasion, Alexander's armies carried Hellenic concepts as far as India in the fourth century BC, laying the ground for a continuing cross-fertilization of ideas. Greek philosophy penetrated Persia, Persian science and mysticism percolated westward. Alexander's military adventures opened up the kind of communication in which the followers of Jesus in Palestine could have had access to the teachings of the Buddha.

Rome's command of the Mediterranean world was a supreme act of constructive conquest. At its height, in the second century AD, the Roman Empire stretched from the Atlantic to Arabia, from the Danube in the north to the shores of Tripoli. Roman hegemony created the conditions for a cultural exchange without precedent in history, before or since. Spaniard and Jew, Gaul and Egyptian, Briton and Greek, German and Berber, Arab and African, Persian and Basque, blackamoor and barbarian mingled in the Empire, exchanging goods and ideas, religions and literature, philosophies, politics, and art.

As conquerors, Romans were at once arrogant and tolerant. Confident in the superiority of their civilization, they allowed all manner of subcultures to flourish. The Pax Romana, backed by force of arms, was a shield to hundreds of societies and a fortress against the tribal chaos of the world beyond Rome's walls. The great cities of the Empire, from Britain's York to Judea's Jerusalem, were connected by a network of protected highways. "These roads united the subjects of the most distant provinces by an easy and familiar intercourse," [154] Edward Gibbon pointed out in his famous history. And Roman citizens spread out across the empire, taking root in many lands. "Wheresoever the Roman conquers he inhabits," [155] said the Roman philosopher, Lucius Annaeus Seneca.

By the spread of settlement, Romans integrated the Mediterranean world into a single, well-governed system. Extending this rule was Rome's greatest civilizing achievement. Other civilizations will measure the pathways of the sky, or forecast the rising of the stars, Virgil wrote in the *Aeneid,* [156] but Rome's concern was to rule the nations under law.

After Rome, the most culturally productive Mediterranean conquest was carried out by Islam in the seventh and eighth centuries. The social mix of Moor, Christian and Jew under Muslim rule extending from the Middle East along the north African coast and across the Straits of Gibraltar into Spain was extraordinarily fertile. In Arab Al-Andalus (southern Spain), for example, it generated superb universities at Cordoba, Seville and Granada, creating a cultural amalgam that generated Islamic Hellenists such as Avicenna, a disciple of Galen, the physician of antiquity, and Hebraic Neoplatonists such as Moses Maimonides and Moses de Leon, author of the *Zohar,* one of the major books of the mystical Kabbala. At the same time, the agricultural technologies developed in Mesopotamia and Persia transformed the rocky hillsides of Andalusia, elaborating the aqueduct systems built by Roman engineers centuries earlier.

In the centuries that followed, the Norman conquest of England in 1066 fused a Latin-based language powerful in concepts with an Anglo-Saxon tongue rich in direct expression, making English one of the most subtle and flexible languages in the world. Similarly, the Mughal seizure of power in northern India in 1526 generated a superbly sensual flowering of poetry, painting and architecture, epitomized by the Taj Mahal at Agra, where Hindu and Persian-Islamic sensibilities mingled in an imagined replica of God's throne in Paradise.

In all these instances, where conquests were fecund, the host culture always transformed its invaders. *Graecia capta ferum victorem cepit* [157] (Greece taken captive captures her savage conquerors), Horace remarked, contemplating the many ways in which Hellenic art, architecture and philosophy entranced the occupying Romans. But conquests can be truly creative only if the victors open themselves to the genius of the vanquished. They are destructive when the victors destroy the vanquished, literally or culturally, and lose the opportunity to enrich and enlarge their own societies.

In this regard, Christians proved to be generally less open-minded as conquerors than Muslims. Where eclectic Islam happily, even greedily, absorbed the art, thought and manners of its subject peoples, Christianity more often than not crushed them beneath the unholy trinity of creed, cannon and cash. In the Americas, in Africa, in Asia and Australasia, missionaries, militaries, and merchants carrying the banner of Jesus ruthlessly exploited or eliminated native civilizations.

Spaniards flattened the cities of the Aztecs and the Incas, melted down their marvelous golden artifacts, and reduced their peoples to servitude. Englishmen, Frenchmen and Dutchmen wiped out native Americans from the Caribbean to the Arctic Circle, and refused to learn anything from the indigenous people's integration with the natural landscape. In Africa, the rapine included a massive and unbelievably cruel capture of slaves for transportation to the Americas. However, even this cruel action had its benefits, such as the marvelous synthesis of new musical forms in the New World.

\*   \*   \*

Apart from its role in advancing civilization through conquest, armed conflict often has tonic purposes that invigorate  social progress. Writing in early 1941, with Hitler's armies in control of all of Western Europe, American sociologist Robert Park marveled at the extraordinary effort men put into warfare; how it spurred social integration and subdued tensions within the community; how, in wartime, social solidarity intensifies, people of all classes and conditions find common ground, and collaboration reaches a peak. "Into war - a great war, a total war - man puts all he has," Park wrote: "his wealth, his science, his indomitable will, and eventually his very existence." [158]

War reverses all values, Erich Fromm observed. It "encourages deep-seated impulses, such as altruism and solidarity, to be expressed - impulses that are stunted by the principles of egotism and competition that peacetime life engenders in modern man... While a soldier fights the enemy for his life, he does not have to fight the members of his own group for food, medical care, shelter, clothing." [159] Elaborating the theme that violence can help integrate a community, Fromm insisted on a distinction between what he termed "benign" and "malignant" aggression. Benign aggression is "a phylogenetically programmed impulse to attack when vital interests are threatened." [160] However, whether any violence is malignant or benign in its effects depends on the existential situation in which it occurs.

What biologists call "cooperation-for-conflict" has been a prime condition for survival and cultural advance from the beginning of history. In the *Descent of Man*, Charles Darwin pointed out that warfare energizes mankind's unique capacity for complex cooperation and group discipline. "The advantage which disciplined soldiers have over undisciplined hordes follows chiefly from the confidence which each man feels in his comrades," [161] Darwin noted. A people capable of such discipline and cooperation would likely be victorious over others, and in turn be themselves overcome by some other tribe still more highly endowed. "Thus the social and moral qualities would tend slowly to advance and be diffused throughout the world." [162]

In truth, what we call civilization - the creation of complex, cooperative societies with strong social and ethical codes - is no enemy to war. On the contrary, the more civilized man has become, the bloodier are his wars. The Greece of the Golden Age, in the fifth and fourth centuries BC, was a country of almost constant combat, internal and external. In Ancient Rome, the centuries just before and after the birth of Christ, the peak period of its power and culture, were also the most turbulent in its history. The 1600s in Europe, the era of Newton, Copernicus and Galileo, was the era of the brutal Thirty Years War. And no century in the history of humanity has been bloodier, or more scientifically and technologically inventive, than the twentieth.

"The climax of Greek civilization was reached in the terrible epoch of the Peloponnesian War; the most brilliant period of Augustus followed immediately after the Roman civil wars and proscriptions," wrote the nineteenth century French historian Joseph de Maistre. "The French genius was bred by the wars of the League, and was polished by the wars of the Fronde. All great men of the time of Queen Anne [1665-1714] were born amidst a great political commotion. In brief, they say that blood is a fertilizer of the plant of Genius." [163]

Sociologist Pitirim Sorokin noted that, in the history of a nation, most of the periods of its political, social, economic, moral, and mental effervescence, the height of its grandeur, power, magnificence and genius, were usually also the periods marked by high levels of militarism and warfare. Sorokin hastened to add that not every epoch of great belligerency was necessarily one of grandeur and blooming; nor did it mean that war was the main or general cause of scientific progress. But, in his view, the frequent confluence of armed conflict and cultural advance was evident. [164]

Darwin made a further point about the formative role of conflict in human evolution: by standing, walking and running upright, men's hands were freed for wielding weapons, which in turn advanced mankind's manual dexterity, his remarkable eye-hand coordination and his consequent development of elaborate tools.

The doubling in the size of our ancestor's brains, occurring in a relatively short evolutionary span, is very likely a direct result of warfare and its imperative for complex collaborations. Human brains not only increased in volume, they also reorganized the neural tracts and the nuclei that facilitate the interaction of their various parts. The cerebellum, which helps integrate fine motor movements and the response to external stimuli, grew larger and more efficient. "Baboons and chimpanzees and gorillas emerged from the Pleistocene peacefully - with the brains of baboons, chimpanzees and gorillas," wrote biologist Robert Bigelow, while big-brained humans were primed for combat. "*Cooperation* is the secret of success in war," Bigelow added, "and cooperation requires *brains*." [165]
In truth, wherever human societies emerged into history, whether in Egypt, Mesopotamia, Anatolia, Greece, Britain, Scandinavia, China, Mexico or Peru, they were accompanied by a loud clash of arms.

A striking and ironic instance of the ways in which war enhances human cooperation and stimulates complex endeavors is evident in the development of that most destructive of all military inventions, the nuclear weapon. It was only under the intense stimulus of war that such an array of talents - from leading scientists in the field of atomic physics down through engineers, administrators, constructors and manufacturers, on to thousands of unskilled workers - could have combined to produce such an amazing technology in so short a time. "A hydrogen bomb is an example of mankind's enormous capacity for friendly cooperation," Bigelow observed. "Without this high level of cooperation no hydrogen bomb could be built. But without an equally high potential for ferocity, no hydrogen bomb ever *would* be built." [166]

The atomic bomb, though originally intended for destruction in the exigencies of war, has had several positive fallouts. Its technology laid the basis for the postwar nuclear power industry which, for all its problems, has provided us with a great new source of energy to replace the fossil fuels that pollute the earth's atmosphere. More dramatically, the invention of a range of nuclear weaponry capable of enormous destruction has all but eliminated the possibility of massive global conflicts of the type that has ravaged humanity twice in this century. Without the presence of the hydrogen bomb, and the ballistic missiles that can carry it vast distances, the Soviet Union and the United States might well have gone to war several times in the past half century. As it is, in Korea, Vietnam, Cuba and Eastern Europe, both major nuclear powers drew back from the brink of an all-out conflict that could have led to the end of civilization.

For the first time in history mankind has made weapons that could destroy civilization - weapons that are essentially unusable, except as a massive deterrent. However, limited local wars, with their creative or destructive potential, are still very much part of the human scenario. And the contribution of military technologies to advances in civilian science and industry continues even in times of peace.

\*   \*   \*

We are without doubt the most cooperative and most combative animals that have ever inhabited the earth, and there is plenty of evidence to show that war - history at high speed - often spurs rapid economic and social advance. For example, in the aftermath of World War Two, the U.S. changed from an isolationist Atlantic power struggling to recover from a major economic depression into a global superpower with a general standard of living higher than any nation in history.

From 1950 to the early 1970s real median family income in the U.S. doubled - an astonishing achievement. In 1940 more than a fifth of the U.S. population lived on farms; fewer than a third of those farms had electric lights and only one farm in ten had flush toilets. Today, a tiny fraction of Americans is engaged in agriculture, and U.S. farming is the world's most mechanized, efficiently providing relatively cheap food for an expanding population.

Before World War Two more than half of all American families rented their homes, most of which lacked central heating. Today, two-thirds of American families own their houses or apartments, and the size of the average U.S. house has almost tripled, from 800 to around 2,300 square feet. With the average household reduced from 4.2 to 2.3 people, each member of the family now enjoys far more room space than any earlier generation.

The unprecedented affluence spurred by the postwar stimulation of the U.S. economy is evident in many things Americans now take for granted. Air travel has become commonplace, increasing from around three million passengers a year before 1940 to 1990's 466 million. In the same period telephone calls jumped from 100 million a year to 1.3 billion, and the number of students in college has grown almost four times. Even health coverage, currently the subject of heated debate and concern, has zoomed. Before World War Two barely a tenth of the U.S. population had health insurance, compared to over three-quarters today.

World War Two spurred many deep economic and social changes. It laid the foundations for an interdependent global economy that has brought unprecedented and widespread prosperity to the technologically advanced countries of Europe, America, Asia, and Australasia (though it still has to solve the problem of helping the world's most economically undeveloped nations to share in this new affluence). It helped provoke social progress, such as the extension of economic equality to women, and, in the United States, full civil rights to long disadvantaged minorities such as African-Americans and native Americans. The fight for social justice stimulated by the war led to the extension of welfare programs in most Western democracies, even in vehemently anti-socialist America. The crude capitalism of the 1920s and 1930s, with its pseudo-Darwinian credo of the survival of the fittest and the victimization of the powerless, became more balanced by some sense of responsibility for those whom prosperity passes by.

Women have been among the greatest beneficiaries of the war-enhanced economy. Apart from the obvious advances in women's rights and opportunities, the housewife has acquired a host of labor-saving devices that liberate her from her mother's and grandmother's mind-numbing drudgery. Domestic machines - washers, driers, dishwashers, refrigerators, freezers, microwave ovens - poured from wartime factories converted to peacetime production. The modern consumerist society moralists deplore, and most everyone enjoys, was born on the battlefields of the Atlantic and the Pacific.

Apart from the social and material advances stimulated by World War Two, the moral issues resolved on its battlefields were profound. To begin with, the basic right of self-defence against aggression was forcefully reinforced. The Allied role in World War Two was, by general consent, a just response to ruthless aggression. "We are fighting to re-establish the reign of law and to protect the liberties of small countries," Winston Churchill said in a wartime speech. "Our defeat would mean an age of barbaric violence, and would be fatal, not only to ourselves, but to the independent life of every small country in Europe." [167]

Whatever the political and economic confusions and tensions that led up to it - and there were many - the Second World War involved a massive assault upon the virulent cancer of fascism corrupting the globe's body politic. The fight was bloody in the extreme. More than forty million soldiers and civilians died, and military terrorism, such as the saturation bombing of cities, was perpetrated by both sides. But this terrible toll was, it seems, the only way to attack the cancerous cells polluting the bloodstream of the modern world. "Where the methods of justice cease, war begins," [168] declared the seventeenth century Dutch jurist, Hugo Grotius. But, he cautioned, the degree of violence must match the extremity of the threat or the repression, and it must establish its moral necessity.

A recent example of a war with a strong justification was the 1971 Indian invasion of East Pakistan, now named Bangladesh. The Bengalis of East Pakistan, suffering massacres by a West Pakistan army of Punjabis, fled to neighboring India by the millions. Their stories of atrocities inflamed Indian opinion, adding fuel to a long, hot antagonism between India and Pakistan. Finally, after running out of diplomatic options, the Indian Army launched a two-week war surgical war to drive the Pakistani forces from Bangladesh. The Indians then withdrew, leaving the Bengalis to establish their own independent state.

The elements of justice were clear in that instance. There was a condition of brutal suppression, followed by the passionate appeal of the persecuted for help from a powerful neighbor. India accomplished the liberation of Bangladesh as swiftly as possible, then pulled out. Of course, India's motives were not completely altruistic; but politics, and its handmaiden, war, is always the art of the relative. It is in calculating the relativity of violent actions in response to violent situations that their necessity must be measured.

The notion of a justified military action was invoked in the concept of Righteous War, formulated by the fifth century BC Chinese philosopher, Mo Tzu. Suppose, he said, that there is a country which is being persecuted and oppressed by its rulers, and a sage prince, "in order to rid the world of this pest raises an army and sets out to punish the evil-doers." [169] The fault will come, Mo Tzu wrote, if the victorious prince, following the pacifist doctrine of Confucius, fails to pursue and totally destroy the enemy. If this happens, "the violent and disorderly will escape with their lives and the world will not be rid of its pest." [170] The truth of this statement was recently revealed in the 1991 Gulf War, where the Iraqui dictator Saddam Hussein, a major pest, was allowed to hold onto power after his army was decimated.

Getting rid of dangerous factions has long been the basis for righteous wars and justified rebellions. In the sixth century BC, at the dawn of the Western democratic tradition in the era of Solon, the great Athenian lawgiver, Hellenic peasant farmers rose up in brave insurrections against greedy landlords. "How and why such spirit entered the breasts of these impoverished visionaries is one of the great unanswered historical questions... We are the beneficiaries of their remarkable refusal to be passive victims." [171] Revolutionary war, Friedrich Engels declared, "is the midwife of every old society which is pregnant with the new... it is the instrument by the aid of which social movement forces its way through and shatters the dead, fossilized, political forms." [172]

The American Revolution was a valid rebellion against a colonial power that would not yield to either civilian riots or peaceful persuasion. Americans began their rebellion only after exhausting all peaceful means to bring about social and political justice. In 1778, while the American colonies were fighting for their independence from Britain, Thomas Paine wrote that "if there ever was a *just* war since the world began, it is this in which America is now engaged." [173]

The American and French revolutions - the political introductions to the modern world - shattered fossilized political forms that resisted change by peaceful means. But the two conflicts had very different characters and effects, and these differences throw a sharp light on the role of violence as a force for political and social evolution in different places and at different times.

The American Revolution established a working democracy whose basic institutions have endured through extraordinary expansions of territory and population, and the radical transformation of an agrarian economy into an industrial one. Though largely led by those who considered themselves landed or propertied gentlemen, the American revolution prepared the ground for a society that is to a large degree socially, if not economically, classless. The concept of upward mobility, of the supremacy of success, overrode the inherited English precedence of birth and breeding.

Virtue and talent are the grounds of a natural aristocracy, Thomas Jefferson wrote to John Adams in 1813, and revolt against the "louts and rascals" who constantly attempted to distort the character of his beloved republic was a recurring necessity. Several years after the new United States of America was a fact, the aging patrician author of the Declaration of Independence remarked to James Madison, that "a little rebellion, now and then, is a good thing, and as necessary in the political world as storms in the physical." [174] In Alexis de Tocqueville's perceptive comment, Americans "consider society as a body in a state of improvement... in which nothing is, or ought to be permanent." [175]

In the United States, the rebellion sought the overthrow of a distant colonial power. Once this yoke was shed, once the last Redcoat retreated to Canada or sailed for home, a native pragmatism allowed the Americans to adjust their society slowly. True, they permitted slavery to continue, made no move to modify a genocidal hatred of the native peoples, and kept women politically powerless; but overall the civic culture that followed independence from Britain was a remarkable advance in the history of human freedom.

By contrast, in France, things changed rapidly and ruthlessly. The monarch was murdered and institutions trashed. Even the standard calendar, dating its origin from the birth of Christ, was abolished in an abrupt fervor for radical renewal. 1789 was the year the French invented the modern meaning of the word "revolution," in the sense of the mass uprising of one social class against another. 1793 was the year they gave us the term "terror," in the particular political sense in which we now use the word. "French Revolution means here the open, violent rebellion and victory of disemprisoned anarchy against corrupt, worn-out authority," [176] Thomas Carlyle wrote in his classic work on the French Revolution. It was a "transcendental phenomenon, overstepping all rules and experience, the crowning experience of our modern time."

*The Marsellaise*, the French Revolution's anthem, inspired citizens seeking social reform in Britain, Napoleon's chief enemy. Its stirring tune and lyrics moved Garibaldi's men in Italy, along with revolutionaries in Hungary, Germany, Austria and Spain, down to the anti-Tsarist Russian rebels of 1905 and 1917. But, unlike the American Revolution - which was more a rebellion than a true revolution - the French Revolution did not establish an enduring social or political framework. Napoleon soon distorted its aims with his imperial dreams, and the old monarchy was reintroduced after his final defeat at Waterloo.

However, the French Revolution has retained a mythical power as an icon of social renewal that is inspirational to this day. The notion of a spontaneous egalitarian democracy based on universal suffrage, sprung from popular opinion, guarded by a free press, was dramatized in France in the last decades of the eighteenth century. Carlyle put his finger on the mythic persistence of the memory of the French Revolution when he wrote that, "whatsoever is cruel in the panic frenzy of twenty-five million men, whatsoever is great in the simultaneous death-defiance of twenty-five million men, stand here in abrupt contrast; all of black on one side, all of bright on the other." [177]

\* \* \*

Jefferson's remark that a little rebellion now and then is a good thing echoes on through American history. Only three years after the American colonies achieved their independence, the turbulent 1786 Shays Rebellion influenced the Philadelphia legislature in reforming intolerable taxation, and had a powerful impact on the following year's Constitutional Convention. In the pre-Civil War condition of slavery in the American South ex-slave Frederick Douglass declared that "Every slavehunter who meets a bloody death in his infernal business is an argument in favor of the manhood of our race." [178] More recently, U.S. labor's often ferocious battles with mine and factory owners in the 1930s changed the character of U.S. capitalism. And the burning of Harlem and Watts helped spark the advance of black civil rights in the 1960s and early '70s.

In 1969, at the height of the civil protests in the U.S. against the Vietnam War - in the midst of student sit-ins and the rioting in Harlem, Watts, Detroit and other major cities echoing with cries of *Burn, Baby Burn!* - Supreme Court Justice William O. Douglas declared that "We must realize that today's Establishment is the new George III. Whether it will adhere to its tactics, we do not know. If it does, the redress, honored in tradition, is revolution." [179]

It is striking that, in the U.S., rebellions have generally taken a social rather than an overtly political form of action. In America's supposedly classless society the intensely politicized class conflicts that have racked European nations have seldom occurred. Americans have no real notions of the proletariat or the bourgeoisie to inflame their banners of revolt.

Take the case of African-Americans; their deep and persistent grievances have seldom been cast in cogently political terms. It took the ascendance of Malcolm X and the Black Panthers in the 1960s to give the black struggle for true equality in America an ideology of rebellion. Malcolm X's political vehemence, a tonic counterpoint to Martin Luther King's social non-violence, was a major factor in impelling the white power structure to pass landmark civil rights legislation in 1964 and '65. Behind the ballot is the bullet, his message implied, so you better choose the Nice Negro over the Black Prince at his back. For many African-Americans, Malcolm X remains a symbol of true black power, "our living black manhood," [180] in actor Ossie Davis's graveside phrase.

After Malcolm X, the politics of revolt were most strongly formulated by the Black Panther Party. Created in Oakland, California, in 1966, by two young men, Huey P. Newton and Bobby Seale, the movement spread across the U.S. like wildfire in the following few years. By 1968 the Panthers claimed five thousand members in Chicago alone. Black people are a true political nation in revolt, Seale emphasized, since blacks share a common economic oppression.

The Black Panther's violent stance was dramatized in a shoot-out with Oakland police in October 1967, in which Newton was wounded and an officer was killed.

However, the Panthers were far less successful than Malcolm X in raising the consciousness of African-Americans and stirring the conscience of whites, for several reasons. Externally, the Panthers were continually harassed by the Federal Bureau of Investigation; internally, many of its leaders were corrupt and despotic, or, like Newton himself, were addicted to drugs. But perhaps the deeper reason is that, since the War of Independence and the American Civil War, political rebellion has never gained wide support in the United States. As remarked above, Americans favor social protest, both violent and nonviolent, as their favored mode of making change happen.

In a modern democratic society, civil structures evolve in a complex fashion. Where autocratic or rigidly hierarchical cultures often require outright rebellion to effect any real change, in a modern democracy the means to social and political evolution tend to be more flexible, diverse, and informal. For instance, the movement for women's political rights in the early decades of this century welled up in a largely spontaneous manner. Similarly, antagonistic notions concerning homosexuals began to alter in many unstructured encounters between gays and straights in the decades between the 1960s and the 1980s, finally achieving the codification of homosexuals' right to equality under the law.

Sometimes deep social changes not directly provoked by the economy originate as civic groundswells, surges from the inchoate spring of communal feeling. Such groundswells - which may first become manifest among a particular group of citizens - like the "counterculture" of the 1960s - won't succeed in influencing the deeper currents of social life unless they overflow into a wider pool of general acceptance. This acceptance most often arises from latent pressures bubbling under the surface of fixed attitudes, driven by a widespread feeling of frustration and the growing belief that something must change. In this way, the shock of revolution or rebellion can be avoided.

And there is no doubt that rebellion can be brutal. In his film, *The Battle of Algiers*, Italian director Bruno Pontecorvo included a scene in which a bomb is set off in an Algiers milk bar during the Algerians' struggle for independence from France in the 1950s. As the device explodes, a jukebox is flung out into the street; blood, chunks of flesh and strips of clothing fill the screen. Through the dense white smoke the audience hears men shouting hoarsely, women weeping hysterically. One girl, her arm torn off, blunders about wildly, out of control. However, it was scenes such as these that finally forced the French to end their colonial regime in Algeria.

Similar horrors helped coerce Rhodesian whites into surrendering my home country, now Zimbabwe, to its native inhabitants, following a bloody, seven-year civil war between black guerilla forces and a white minority government determined to maintain a racist society. In 1973, when I visited Rhodesia after a twenty-year absence, a snapshot of a blonde bathing beauty in a skimpy bikini shared the front page of my old hometown newspaper, the *Bulawayo Chronicle*, with a photo of a mutilated victim of "terrorists." This crude juxtaposition offered a chilling lesson in the harsh realities underpinning the privileges of a dying colonial society.

Despite the refusal of almost every country to recognize the Rhodesia regime, and the imposition of international sanctions by the United Nations, the whites were determined to defend their privileges, up to a point. "We'll hang on here till our swimming pools are filled with blood," one former schoolfriend told me. "Then, maybe, we'll think again." In the event, the will of the whites snapped well before the war poisoned their pools.

Objectively, a great deal depends upon the question of equivalence in such situations. To be justifiable, the rebels' use of violence must be appropriate to the intractable and oppressive character of the political opposition it encounters. The measure of the means employed by an entrenched power to suppress a majority, or large minority, of its citizens or subjects must be the measure of the violence resorted to by those in revolt against its authority. Rebel terror may only respond to actual state terror, murder for murder, wound for wound.

In this context, the bombing of the federal building in Oklahoma City by right-wing extremists in 1995, which killed 168 people, was an act of political destruction way in excess of any real repression. The U.S. federal authorities are plainly not the "jack-booted thugs" fantasized by an official of the National Rifle Association, even though their lethal 1993 attack on the Branch Davidian compound in Waco, Texas, was criminal in its ineptitude.

However, when political protest confronts a ruthless and un-yielding established power, non-violent methods are bound to fail. The strategy of *satyagraha*, passive resistance, worked for Ghandi and his followers in British India because Whitehall refused to use the barbaric tactics the Nazis employed to subdue resistance in World War Two.

But even the saintly Ghandi understood the limits of nonvio-lence. "I do believe that where there is only a choice between cow-ardice and violence I would advise violence," the Mahatma said. [181] Similarly, theologian Reinhold Niebuhr declared that "The differ-ences between violent and non-violent methods of coercion and re-sistance are not so absolute that it would be possible to regard vio-lence as a morally impossible instrument of change... The advan-tages of non-violent methods are very great but they must be prag-matically considered in the light of circumstances." [182]

*Pragmatically considered in the light of circumstances...* This is the crux of the matter in distinguishing justified from unjustified rebellions, as it is in distinguishing between the creative and de-structive elements in most human actions, from the political to the personal. Albert Camus put it this way: "Absolute nonviolence is the negative basis of slavery and its acts of violence; systematic vio-lence positively destroys the living community and the existence we must receive from it. To be fruitful, these two ideas must estab-lish final limits." [183]

Within such limits, the authority to impose violent sanctions to maintain power is a legitimate function of the law and its organs of justice, the German philosopher and social critic Walter Benjamin argued. "All [legitimate] violence as a means is either lawmaking or law-preserving," [184] he observed, and any democratic govern-ment should never forget that its moral and social authority ulti-mately rests on the sanctioned violence of its police, armed forces, and penal system. "When the consciousness of the latent presence of violence in a legal institution disappears, the institution falls into decay." [185]

As an example of such decadence, Benjamin pointed to the fatal impotence of Germany's pre-Nazi Weimar Republic, which lost sight of this crucial fact. In this lapse, the Weimar legislators fell prey to extremists of the right and left, who had a more instinctive grasp of the fundamental truth that, "in the exercise of violence over life and death more than any other legal act, law reaffirms itself." [186]

The ferocities of rebellion can have yet another positive function: in their blood and fire new national identities may be forged. The bombs bursting in air and the rocket's red glare illuminate fresh flags in the dawn's early light.

In Zimbabwe, the symbol of a new aspiration to nationhood was the soapstone bird identified with the Zimbabwe Ruins, a medieval fortress built by African ancestors; the soapstone bird was reborn in blood, and blazoned on the new flag. The rebirth was doubly necessary, since the colonial white regime had attempted to appropriate the artifact as its own trademark.

The role of violence in defining the identity of an infant nation is epitomized in modern times by the State of Israel. Without the many wars against its Arab neighbors, would millions of people of every race and color, whose only common ground is a complex and often conflicting sense of being Jewish, ever have forged an Israeli nationality? Whether one favors the Zionist aspiration or opposes it, it has to be acknowledged that the condition of almost continuous war has generated a powerful sense of Israeli nationhood in a very short time.

The Israeli example is especially illuminating. Here we have a human community that is simultaneously very old and very new. As a culture, Jewishness dates back to the era of Babylon and Pharaonic Egypt. As a race, Jews have long been polyglot, mingled with a multitude of hosts. The Nazi *Der Sturmer* may have tried to invent a hostile Hebrew archetype, but it was a caricature few Jews in Yemen or Morocco would have recognized. As a nation, however, modern Jews are infants. Their national identity was destroyed by the Romans nearly two thousand years ago. Between the fall of the Zealot fortress of Masada in 73 AD and the capture of East Jerusalem by the Israeli army in 1967, Jews seldom had a political identity to match their cultural connection.

Whether Jews and Judaism needed a modern national identity or not is another and far more complex question. What is certain is that Israelis, like so many neophyte communities seeking their own kind of character, would never have achieved it without the creative force of violence.

*   *   *

In the history of Western civilization, two polarities generate much of the positive electricity of political thought and action. One pole is charged with a yearning for individual freedom, for the fullest expression of personal potential within the confines of the community. The other sparks a search for a condition of communal well-being, for what Plato described as "the sacred and golden cord of reason, known as the common law." [187] Power arcs across these poles, switching from one to the other as the current fluctuates over the centuries.

Over time, furies of the mind and heart have energized both the yearning for freedom and the search for a civilized society bound by that golden cord. In their creative forms, these passions constantly challenge the assumptions and constrictions of established social structures. Or they fiercely contest the ways in which men might most effectively erect those structures to serve the general well-being of the society at large. Either way, a constant alertness is critical to the life of the body politic, combating the ever present threat of oppression or functional disjunction.

However, in political life freedom and virtue can never find a permanent balance. As situations change, the fruitful instability of human societies shunts between rivalry and collaboration. What makes a man's behavior political, "is that he rules and obeys, persuades and compromises, promises and bargains, coerces and represents, fights and fears," [188] striving to refine and redefine the workings of the common law in a wide variety of circumstance.

Western concepts of common law have sailed under many flags. They have borne the banner of Plato's "Forms," Saint Augustine's "Divine Ideas," Immanuel Kant's "Kingdom of Ends," Jean Jacques Rousseau's "General Will," the American Revolution's "self-evident truths," The French Revolution's "Liberty, Equality, Fraternity," Friedrich Hegel's "Philosophy of Right," and the modern liberal's common ground or sense of community. Politics is a matter of means and ends, and the notions of a dynamic social equilibrium are constantly redefined as power shifts and aspirations alter under the influence of potent temperaments.

Western civilization's long search for dynamic political systems based on common law owe much to the young Renaissance prince, Cesare Borgia, and Niccolo Machiavelli, the political philosopher who held Borgia up as a model. For many, Borgia and

Machiavelli have a bad reputation, but others give Machiavelli credit for founding the modern discipline of political science.

Macchiavelli praised Borgia for the bold way he employed ruthless action in the service of a communal good. A prince, Machiavelli wrote, should "inspire fear in such a fashion that, if he does not win love, he may escape hate." He must be a lion, but he must also know how to play the fox. "The prince, in short, ought not to quit good courses if he can help it, but should know how to follow evil courses if he must." [189] Driven by a pragmatic wisdom operating in a complex world, Borgia's concept of virtue was rational and empirical, free of special pleading. At its best, the prince's private self-interest fused with the public good to serve a stable social order based on the rule of law.

In a famous example, the Italian ruler subdued the restless cities of the Italian Romagna by a skilful mixture of cruelty and subtlety. Having failed to convince the citizens to settle their disputes by peaceful means, Borgia sent in Ramiro d'Orco, "a man cruel and quick of action," [190] with full powers to do what was needed to impose order.

D'Orco's cruelty was extreme. One day he booted a clumsy young page into the fireplace, pinning him there with a poker until he burned to death. Such barbarity chilled the Romagnans into submission, into what one historian called "comparative tranquility." [191] But after cruelty came justice, and Borgia had d'Orco killed and cut in two, his severed body displayed in the piazza of Cesena. Machiavelli, who witnessed the event, commented tersely: *"La ferocita del quale spettaculo fece quelli populi in uno tempo rimanere satisfatti e stupiti."* [192] ("The ferocity of the spectacle left the crowd simultaneously satisfied and stupified.") In this way, Borgia satisfied the citizens' desire for revenge, purged their hatred, and laid the foundation for a lasting peace.

Machiavelli's thesis of ruthless action in the service of a communal good marked a profound shift of emphasis in a political tradition that went back two thousand years, to Plato, Aristotle, and the Presocratic philosophers. His books, *The Prince* and *Discourses*, defined a sharp split of ethics from politics; ethics, that is, in the sense of abstract laws concerning right and wrong, as against Machiavelli's pragmatic morality in the service of social order. Where the Hellenes, and later the Christians, saw political life as the reflection of an abstract ethical dimension, whether philosophical or di-

89

vine, Machiavelli perceived it as a totally human phenomenon shaped by its own purposes and subject to its own imperatives. How we live is so different from how ethics declares we ought to live, Machiavelli wrote, "that he who studies what ought to be done rather than what is done will learn the way to his downfall rather than to his preservation." [193]

Machiavelli based his political philosophy on empirical fact; in that sense, he made it a science rather than an ideology. In his view, justified violence carries its own moral authority. As the Christian philosopher, Jacques Maritain, remarked, "What others call evil actions may sometimes be the authentically moral behavior of a just man engaged in the complexities of human life." [194] The need for justice may require a relentless energy against wicked and false-hearted enemies, Maritain added, and a lesser evil may be needed to drive out a greater one, to achieve a dynamic balance in the body politic.

Jesus himself announced that he had come not to send peace on earth but a sword, forever damning those unbelieving "swine" before whom pearls of wisdom should never be cast. "All power is given unto me in heaven and in earth," [195] Jesus told his disciples, boasting that his flock, dubbed "the meek," would conquer the world. In *The Gnostic Gospels*, Elaine Pagels argued convincingly that the orthodox Christian gospels were, in effect, war propaganda; since the gospels are the source of Christ's purported preachings, we have to accept them as the basis of his faith.

Like Cesare Borgia, Jesus - in the words recorded by his apostles - clearly grasped the vital role of coercion in the establishment and advancement of a particular communal order. "For I am come to set a man at variance against his father, and the daughter against the mother, and the daughter in law against her mother in law," he declared, "And a man's foes shall be they of his own household."[196] Anyone who offended his disciples should have a millstone hung about his neck and be "drowned in the depth of the sea;" [197] any devotee troubled by doubt should cut off the offending hand or foot, or pluck out his eye if he wanted to avoid being cast into hell fire. "Woe unto the world because of offences!" Jesus thundered to his flock. "Woe to that man by whom the offence cometh!" [198] When Christianity became established in the Roman Empire, and on down through the ages, heretics were mercilessly hounded, and the sword has been integral to the culture of the Church, cutting a bloody swath through legions of perceived enemies.

More recently, Talcott Parsons, one of the dominant figures in post-World War Two American sociology, argued that the role and significance of force in political life has been underplayed by liberal theories of progress and linear evolution. He claimed that these theories refuse to acknowledge that force "frequently attends the `creative' process by which a new value system becomes established in a society through the succession to power of a new elite." [199]

After the American War of Independence, a dynamic balance between high-minded idealism and hard-headed Machiavellian pragmatism was sought by some of the new elite among the Federalist founders of the United States, including James Madison, Alexander Hamilton and John Adams. The American constitutional concept of checks and balances between executive, legislative and judicial centers of power is charged with Machiavelli's pragmatic pessimism, his sense of the creative conflict between lesser and greater evils. If Machiavelli made politics a science, the Federalists put scientific politics to work, to balance the fine but plainly false notions that all men are created equal and are equipped with inalienable rights.

\*   \*   \*

Machiavelli's recognition of the positive role of violence in the service of social order was turned on its head by anarchists and communists in the nineteenth and twentieth centuries. These movements embraced violence as a weapon for revolution, for a continual tide of upheaval in the newly industrialized nations of Europe and America. Revolution is the driving force of history, Karl Marx declared, and communism derived its ultimate authority from its claim to be the solution to "the riddle of history."

In truth, the suffering of working people during the social upheaval and brutal exploitation of the early Industrial Revolution was staggering. Friedrich Engels, Marx's self-described "second violin," detailed this horror in his classic study, *The Condition of the Working Class in England in 1844.* Describing a district in the manufacturing city of Manchester, Engels wrote of a warren of passages and streets covered in grime and filth. A stream weaves through the warren, leaving "a long string of the most disgusting blackish-green slime pools," giving off the stench of "miasmatic gas."

The packed houses are "black, smoky, crumbling, ancient, with broken panes and window frames." Streams of refuse, offal and sewage flow past front doors in these "cattle sheds for human beings." [200]

Children went to work in Manchester's mills and factories at five or six years old. In the adjoining iron and coal mines, which fed the engines of Britain's prosperity as the world's first and leading industrial power, men, women and children crawled through narrow underground tunnels in the semi-dark, emerging after twelve and fourteen-hour days blinking like moles in the pale sunlight. Accidents and explosions were common; tubercolosis, typhus and cholera were rampant, and cheap gin and laudanum, a tincture of opium, provided a degrading escape from the pains of daily life.

In this degraded social context, young Marx found his powerful voice. "The world which bulks between me and the abyss/I will smash to pieces with my enduring curses," [201] he wrote in *Oulanem*, an attempted early tragedy in verse, modeled on Goethe's *Faust.* Political philosophy, in his view, had to be an attack upon the profoundly alienating effects of modern society; a society fractured by forced specialization, economic exploitation, and a sterile split between man's personal and public existence. "The criticism that tackles this state of affairs is engaged in a hand-to-hand battle," [202] Marx declared.

The devil in Marx's political theology was named Money or Capital. "If money...comes into the world with a congenital bloodstain on its cheek," he wrote in *Das Kapital,* "capital comes dripping from head to foot, from every pore, with blood and filth." [203] *Das Kapital,* a penetrating intellectual critique of Victorian capitalism, was shot through with vivid metaphors of an almost biblical iniquity. He described the English working man's daily loaf as being adulterated with "human perspiration mixed with the discharge of abscesses, cobwebs, dead black-beetles and putrid German yeast." [204]

Marx's sense of outrage stoked the fire of his thought; but through the flames he had a vision of a utopian society in which the division of life and labor demanded by industrialized economies would give way to a time of wholeness. The separation of home and workplace, the social schizophrenia that splits a mechanized society, would vanish. As in pre-industrial times, families would live, work and play together. Each person would be supplied in accordance with his needs, and contribute to the common pool according to his abilities. The insatiable urge to produce and consume that had come to rule people's lives would give way to a realm of unstressed ease free of envy and desire. Revolutionary violence, which Engels called "the midwife of progress," would blast open the path to this utopia.

At bottom, Marx's intellectual fury sprang from a passionate search for ways to be human in the Machine Age, and his core message still has great moral energy. Marx, a descendant of rabbis and a child of the Enlightenment, was trained in what the early nineteenth century termed Natural Philosophy, a discipline with a strong sense of moral purpose.

The failures of Marxism that followed Marx's death have often been due to the absence of a similar morality in many of his followers. Lenin seized upon obscure Marxist notions, such as the dictatorship of the proletariat, as devices of state power, and doctrinal Marxist-Leninism became a rigid shell devoid of any ethical spirit. Leon Trotsky's cry for World Revolution, engineered by force and subversion, expressed a naked lust for power for its own sake. In Mao Tse Tung's heavy hand, Marxism was reduced to a clutch of pithy Red Book maxims, and Stalin's blunt belief that the state is simply a weapon in the hands of the ruling class, to break the resistance of its enemies, would certainly have made Marx scowl.

The very word "Marxist," coined late in Marx's life, made the man squirm. "If that's what some people mean by Marxism, then I, at least, am not a Marxist," [205] he insisted. Delivering Marx's funeral oration in London's Highgate Cemetery, a tearful Engels claimed that Marx's death would leave a huge void. "Battle was his element," Engels said, "and he battled with a passion and tenacity few could rival." [206] Marx, like Nietzsche, was a self-described "man of calamity," one who believed that the alienating social structures which confine modern man would only be overthrown by a political and social convulsion, propelled by a radical change of heart.

The concept of violence as a positive political and social weapon lies at the heart of the movement known as anarchism. The word itself, from the original Greek *an-arkhos* - anti-ruler - summarizes the movement's vehement opposition to any form of governance that places the demands of society above the absolute right to individual freedom. A Spanish slogan sums up the anarchist sentiment in a sentence: *Paz a los Hombres, Guerra a las Instituciones* (Peace toward People, War Against Institutions).

In the history of anarchism, the act of revolution itself has often seemed the purest form of expression. Yet there has long been a tension between those anarchists who feel that life must be a constant revolt against an oppressive society, and those who emphasize the brotherhood of men living together in simple communities. "We must not suppose that *revolutionary* action is the means of social reform," [207] Pierre Joseph Proudhon said in a letter to Karl Marx - a man he first admired, then disliked. His rival anarchist, the rambunctious Russian nobleman Mikhail Bakunin, trumpeted that "The urge for destruction is also the creative urge!" [208] The anarchist newspaper, *Le Revolte,* founded by Russian Prince Peter Alexeivitch Kropotkin, called for "Permanent revolt by word of mouth, in writing, by the dagger, the rifle and dynamite," [209] and his disciples were eager to oblige.

The murders of President Sadi Carnot of France in 1894, U.S. President William McKinley in 1901, the Empress Elizabeth of Austria and the Prime Minister of Spain, plus a host of failed attempts at assassination, were all anarchist inspired. In Worcester, Massachusetts, Emma Goldman plotted the assassination of Henry Clay Frick, the chairman of the board of the Carnegie Corporation, and an Italian anarchist from Paterson, New Jersey, murdered Italy's King Umberto in 1900. As Europe drifted toward the First World War - a cataclysm whose wholesale slaughter made individual political murders seem trivial - the appeal of anarchism intensified. Georges Clemenceau, French prime minister during World War One, said he was sorry for anyone who hadn't been an anarchist at twenty. In the 1930s another French premier, Leon Blum, remarked that his whole literary generation had been impregnated by anarchist thought.

Georges Sorel, a retired French civil engineer, developed a theory about the myth of violence as a power for social change. Sorel's 1906 book, *Reflections on Violence,* praised the drama of the general strike, comparing it to the early Christian apocalyptic myth of the total ruin of the pagan world. It did not matter that that catastrophe never occurred, Sorel declared; its mythology greatly inspired and focused Christian resolve for centuries. By the same token, the violent general strike, as a revolutionary myth, could create "a body of images capable of evoking instinctively all the sentiments which correspond to the different manifestations of the war" [210] against modern society.

Anarchist mythology, and its political handmaiden, syndical-ism, flourished in Spain up to the time of the country's civil war in the mid 1930s. The 1909 Barcelona revolt, known as the *Semana Tragica*, was described by one participant as "A week of intoxica-tion, of holy rage, seeing that the fury of the masses was justified by a hundred centuries of misery, oppression and endurance." [211] Fran-cisco Ferrer, an early Spanish anarchist executed for his beliefs, spoke of "ideas of destruction in the mind." [212]

Today the cry, *Peace to People, War against Institutions!* still carries a strong emotional appeal for those who feel that an over-organized and culturally abstract industrial society has polluted the earth and destroyed the humanity of our cities. But to be creative rather than destructive in its ends, such violence must be an appro-priately considered response to the social and political context it is challenging.

In fact, an honest, hard-headed pragmatism is crucial in consid-ering the circumstantial justification of any act of rebellion, the right-eousness of any war, the creativity of any conquest. At the same time it must be recognized that the particular phenomenon we call *revolution*, though often rooted in specific social, political and his-torical grievances, is also driven by a deeper, totally unpragmatic purpose. A true revolution, as opposed to a rebellion or revolt, is always charged with a sense of cosmic injustice way beyond the special situation it seeks to change.

Revolutionary upheavals seek to turn things around, to stand circumstances on their heads, to challenge every assumption, from the divinity of the gods to the humanity of men. They are tragic protests against the Fate Beethoven yearned to seize by the throat, the political equivalent of Oedipus blinding himself, of Quixote set-ting out to battle windmill giants, of Ahab's threat to strike the sun itself. They are, in short, yet another expression of our urge to chal-lenge heaven. "The spirit of revolution lies wholly in man's protest against the human condition," Camus wrote. "A revolution is al-ways carried out against the gods - from that of Prometheus on-wards. It is a protest which man makes against his destiny." [213]

Simon Bolivar remarked that revolution is a protest which may be ultimately as futile as plowing the sea. But it is a profound com-plaint mankind must make over and over as we navigate the oceans of eternity.

# 6
# the struggle in the cage

At dawn on January 22, 1991, a trio of U.S. F-117 Stealth fighters, attached to the United Nations' force attacking Iraq during the Persian Gulf War, zoomed down on the city of Mosul. With deadly accuracy the fighters aimed their laser-guided missiles at a series of technological targets, including a power station, a communications center and a suspected underground nuclear weapons facility.

The explosions were devastating, rocking the towers of the minarets, sending shock waves out into the countryside surrounding the ancient city on the Tigris River. The man-made thunder shook the earth and the early morning sky was brilliant with manufactured lightning.

A few miles south, in the village of Hassuna, perched on the highlands overlooking the Tigris, farmers paused for a moment to stare at the pyrotechnic display in the sky, their hoes poised over primitive irrigation canals cut in the hard clay. The farmers listened intently to the rolling thunder of the explosions, feeling the reverberations in their bones. Ears cocked, they worried about the effect of all this uproar on the crops of wheat and barley sown in the previous fall.

12,000 years or so ago in fertile highland valleys such as this human beings first began to radically alter their given relationship with the natural world. By domesticating sheep and goats and planting and harvesting edible grass seeds, men, alone among all of the earth's creatures, began to manipulate and combat nature rather than merely submit to its moods. In this, they were following the ambition, expressed in Genesis, to subdue the earth and take dominion over every living thing. Thus human beings began their long struggle to conquer nature and gain mastery of the planet.

Today, in the technologically advanced areas of the globe, mankind has won major victories in the war against nature's three main elements: time, distance, climate. We can communicate instantaneously with anyone anywhere; we can travel around the world in a matter of hours; we can build vast, airconditioned cities in the swamp or desert. And the creation of tremendous power sources, plus the insight given by modern physics into the heart of nature's own energy creation, have hastened the radical refiguring of the earth in man's image. The ancient agricultural realm, dominated by the seasons and the caprice of natural phenomena, has been essentially mastered, and its old gods have been toppled.

The mission of men, Henry David Thoreau remarked in his mid-nineteenth-century journals, "seems to be, like so many busy demons, to drive the forest all out of the country, from every solitary beaver-swamp and mountainside, as soon as possible." [214] Describing the ruthless attack of the new railroad system on the ancient pastoral landscape of mid-Victorian Britain, Charles Dickens wrote of tracks "piercing through the heart of every obstacle... through the fields, through the woods, through the corn, through the hay, through the chalk, through the mould, through the clay, through the rock... onward and onward ever." It was, Dickens said, "as if the sun itself had given in." [215]

Life is primarily a struggle for energy, declared the nineteenth century Austrian physicist, Ludwig Boltzmann. [216] From James Watt's invention of an efficient steam engine to contemporary rocket boosters capable of blasting through the earth's gravity, the creation of ever more powerful sources of energy have freed us to travel beyond our planet's atmosphere. And the forces released in a nuclear explosion are a quantum leap into yet another realm of power. In the particle accelerators that "smash" atoms, hundreds of billions of electron volts of energy are generated; for a fraction of a second, charged subatomic particles, spun by huge electromagnets in cyclotrons, collide at speeds approaching that of light, at temperatures approximating the fires of the sun.

The Renaissance philosopher, Francis Bacon, hailed the figure of the scientist whose ideas have generated the concepts and technologies that have effected our victory over the natural world as "the hero who put nature on the rack and compels her to bear witness...the propagator of man's empire over the universe, the champion of liberty, the conqueror and subduer of necessities." [217]

However, having subdued nature's necessities, we have invented others of our own, and our remarkable victory over the natural world has had an ironic consequence. The technologies that are our weapons in that triumph have generated an autonomous momentum, an independent forward thrust that threatens to run away with us. In effect, they have come to rule our lives just as ruthlessly as raw nature once did, and we are now as subject to the imperatives of our own technology as we ever were to nature's will. In a striking passage in *The Protestant Ethic and the Spirit of Capitalism*, Max Weber declared that the modern economic order determines "the lives of all who are born into this mechanism...with irresistible force." Mechanized society, which should lie upon modern man's shoulders like a light cloak, has become a burden, for "fate decreed that the cloak should become an iron cage." [218]

Driven toward a future charged with uncertainties, haunted by a deepening sense of social and personal alienation, an increasing air of unreality, we struggle for our lives in the iron cage of technological urgency, reaching out through the bars to touch something raw and human, if only to reassure ourselves that we're still flesh and blood.

Our primal desire for something raw and human is evident in our seemingly insatiable craving for violent entertaintment. In almost every living room in the so-called "advanced" world, on every day and every night, TV bullets explode human bodies in great gusts of gore as children and adults alike sit and cheer. On the sports field, our surrogate heroes and villains take blows that knock them head over heels, much to the delight of the audience and the spectators. Modern fans want to see limbs broken and noses mashed. They howl for blood, cheer the scraps that erupt between players, and gloat gleefully as bones crunch on the football field, in the hockey rink or boxing ring. If the brutality on the field is too tame, the people in the stands may, like some soccer crowds, tear into one another with furious fists, boots, and even clubs and knives. This bloody lust has even trickled down to young children, who have replaced the complex yet healing terrors of traditional fairy tales with the trashy two-dimensional ferocities of video games.

Is this evidence of our stubborn savagery in the midst of extraordinary technological advance? Or does it answer a need for something direct and basic in a world made obscure by abstract yet confining social and economic consequences? Could it be that, for many sane and sober folk, such intemperate amusements represent a yearning for ways to restore a visceral contact with some true root of feeling in a soul-denying world of arid ambiguities? Could the proxy violence of popular pastimes be a reaction to the relentless forward charge of a culture that cages and separates us from any real experience of community? Is it that, in the rush of technological advance we are driven to ask, like Auden in *The Age of Anxiety*: "Are we simply not wanted at all?"

How else explain the copious brutalities served up in popular diversions in our supposedly highly civilized, relatively prosperous societies, except as a widespread need for an essential, if crude human verity, a gut cry for connection in a world deafened by the buzz and crackle of "progress." The second-hand violence of TV and some sporting events is not creative, in the sense that's been discussed; but it is an instinctive reaction to an alienating condition that discounts our grasp of ourselves as personal and public human beings.

*  *  *

Technology, said the French historian and sociologist Jacques Ellul, "has fashioned an omnivorous world which obeys its own laws and which has renounced tradition. Technique no longer rests on tradition, but rather on previous technical procedures; and its evolution is too rapid, too upsetting to integrate the older traditions." In Ellul's techno-future, "the stains of human passion will be lost amid the chromium gleam. We shall have nothing more to lose, and nothing to win." [219]

Ellul used the word "technique" to define the nature of Weber's cloak-turned-cage condition. Technique, in Ellul's sense, includes the entire technological operation, from the actions of a worker on the assembly line or at the computer terminal to the organizational structure of the corporations and governmental agencies which control and regulate the production and trade of goods and services. This woven web of techniques, taken as a whole, he dubbed the "technical phenomenon."

The technical phenomenon integrates men and women with the

processes and necessities of technology. "It constructs the kind of world the machine needs... It clarifies, arranges and rationalizes; it does in the domain of the abstract what the machine did in the realm of labor. It is efficient and brings efficiency to everything." In the prison of its methods, which must be precisely performed, people become "technologues," operatives programmed to maximize technological imperatives.

The physical rigidities of the old industrial systems familiar to Weber and Ellul have been modified by more supple modern methods of manufacture; the concrete realities of heavy manufacturing have largely given way to the abstract manipulations of information systems. But the emotional sense of being caught in technology's iron cage has become more real than ever. To function in the computerized, robotized modern world we must all, to some extent, become "technologues," run by operations whose true nature and intent few of us can grasp; operations which control us and all too often separate us from any sense of being flesh and blood. "Alienation," Octavio Paz said, "is not only the result of social systems, be they capitalist or socialist, but of the very nature of technology: the new means of communication accentuate and strengthen noncommunication." [220]

The nature of modern work itself, which has increasingly to do with the manipulation and exploitation of various kinds of information, is intangible in its essence. We are given sets of procedures and instructions which, if we do them in the right sequence and absolutely correctly, will make the world go round.

But we are haunted by troubling questions: Do those electronic blips on the computer screen really mean something concrete? Can we who operate the terminals take personal pride in those abstract symbols, that seem to live some inner cyber-life of their own, independent of our souls? Does anyone, even at the highest levels of power, really understand what is happening in the world?

This sense of separation from any emotional connection with something tangible and real now pervades every aspect of modern living. Anyone who drives a freeway or uses an automatic teller machine is operating an abstraction. To navigate a freeway a driver must have a map in his head that connects the diagram of the highway network to the jumble of city streets. If he misses his point of intersection, he may wander the freeways, at a loss to reconnect with the city beyond. At the automatic teller a card holder punches in a sequence of chosen numbers that must be absolutely exact, and waits for the impassive and mysterious machine to reward him with cash, or kick out his card in what seems like cold disgust. Actually, it's even more humiliating to realize that, in accepting or rejecting his piece of plastic, the machine is expressing no value judgment whatever, simply an unquestionable fact.

At an even more complex and remote level, scientific abstractions undermine our intrinsic need to grasp the concrete reality of things. Few laymen really understand what the quark-obsessed physicist or DNA-dissecting microbiologist is up to in his high-energy accelerator or genetic laboratory. We've all had to learn to with a degree of conceptual intangibility our forefathers would find deeply disturbing.

A profound sense of imponderability is exuded by the metaphysics of modern physics. Instead of the ultimate absolutes and final surety the earlier Scientific Age seemed to promise, contemporary physicists inhabit the baffling ambiguities of "relativity" and "uncertainty."

Relativity, in Einstein's famous equation, suggests that there is no fixed reference point anywhere in the universe. The implication is that the laws that govern both mechanics and electromagnetism, mass and energy, are the same, and the mass of any body is a function of its speed. The only absolute we are offered is the velocity of light. Mass and energy are interchangeable; the universe and everything in it is essentially energetic rather than physical.

Uncertainty, embodied in Werner Heisenberg's Uncertainty Principle, states that the position and the momentum of an electron particle can never be determined with total accuracy. This "indeterminacy" has a curious character; the more accurately a particle's position is determined, the less its momentum may be measured. In effect this means that if a physicist knows where an electron is he has no idea of what it is doing; if he knows what it is doing, he can have no notion of where it is. The situation is further complicated by the observation that electromagnetic elements seem to function simultaneously as particles and as waves. Heisenberg himself, in an address he delivered on the Hill of Pnyx in Athens, declared that "In fact the smallest units of matter are not physical objects in the ordinary sense; they are forms, ideas which can be expressed unambiguously only in mathematical language." [221]

In modern quantum theory there is a radical inability to pin things down, said the English physicist, John Polkinghorne. "Quantum theory is both stupendously successful as an account of the small-scale structure of the world and it is also the subject of unresolved debate and dispute about its interpretation. That sounds rather like being shown an impressively beautiful palace and being told that no one is quite sure whether its foundations rest on bedrock or shifting sand." [222] In modern physics, then, the whole concept of reality has been given a provocative twist.

Reality may be even more creatively unstable than Polkinghorne says. According to the increasingly influential conjectures of "string" theory, space and time themselves might be illusory. "String" theory attempts to reconcile the space-time continuum of Einstein's theory of gravity with the contradictory concepts of quantum mechanical theory - an inconsistency that plagues the fundamentals of contemporary physics. As a result, Princeton physicist John Archibald Wheeler explained, the "black holes" posited by Einstein suggest "that space can be crumpled like a piece of paper into an infinitesimal dot, that time can be extinguished like a blown-out flame, and that the laws of physics that we regard as `sacred,' as immutable, are anything but." [223]

According to mathematician James Yorke, sometime head of the Institute for Physical Science and Technology at the University of Maryland, even the boundaries between calm and catastrophe are extraordinarily complex. Physicists and mathematicians want to discover regularities, Yorke said, but the first message is that there is disorder. [224] Yorke is one of the originators of the new "chaos theory," that searches for the patterns of order within disorder. This theory, which might be better named "creative chaos," is essentially a hypothesis about turbulence. It holds that the world is forever in the act of becoming at every dimension, a welter of purposeful chaos on a global scale in which everything, large and small, is vitally interconnected. "In the past, people not mistakenly assumed that the world would always be the same. Today this prognosis is manifestly false; but we are still in the dark about what our world will become." [225]

Though the physicists' concepts of relativity and uncertainty, in their strictly scientific sense, seem highly theoretical, their philosophical implications have deeply penetrated the modern consciousness. Since no judgments may be absolute, and every observer affects the object of his observation just by considering it, what we glean of modern physics leads us to the feeling that relativity and uncertainty are inherent in both the human and the natural condition.

Norbert Wiener, father of the new science of cybernetics - the theory of communication and control mechanisms in both living beings and machines - predicted that sometime soon the human brain itself will be replaced by a new order of electro-mechanical evolution. He suggested that humanity, as we have long conceived it, is merely a stage in the advance of the universal Great Mind. "The world of the future will be an ever more demanding struggle against the limits of our intelligence," Wiener wrote, "not a comfortable hammock in which we can lie down to be waited upon by our robot slaves." [226]

The idea that we will be driven to the wall by the inventions of our own intelligence is a deeply troubling notion, but ideas have long had explosive consequences. In fact, the furies of the mind that now threaten to burst the boundaries of our brains have, historically, been among the most forceful anti-nature weapons in the human armory.

For example, in the cultural upheaval that accompanied the rise of Renaissance humanism and its challenge to the established church, radical thinkers rallied the forces of intellectual violence against those who entrenched themselves in divine - that is, nature's - authority. Antagonists on both sides of the conflict attacked and defended forcefully. Paracelsus, considered the founder of modern chemistry, publicly set fire, in Basle's central market, to the books of Galen, the physician of antiquity, and Avicenna, his famous medieval Islamic disciple. On the other side, the Roman Inquisition burned the mystical astronomer Giordano Bruno to death in Venice in 1600 for supposed heresy, and brought Galileo to trial before a Papal court on a similar charge.

Advances in astronomy struck at the heart of the feudal world view that ruled the European mental and spiritual order up to the fifteenth and sixteenth centuries. The observations and hypotheses of Copernicus, Kepler and Galileo displaced the earth from its ancient position at the center of the heavens. In the fusion of Christian theology and Aristotelian philosophy that was Medieval Europe's fundamental faith, the supreme status of the earth in the heavens was crucial. To challenge it was to dethrone God and his vicar the

Pope, and to demolish the established architecture of the world. "The feudal past was indeed violently repudiated," wrote J.D. Bernal, the British historian of science. "The first phase of the Scientific Revolution was mainly a destructive one in the field of ideas." [227]

1543 was a dangerous year for the tottering structure of Gothic beliefs. In that year two major scientific books attacked the old religio-philosophical constructs at their roots. Copernicus published *De Revolutionibus Orbium Coelestium*, detailing the rotation of the earth on its axis and its motion around a fixed sun; and the Italian doctor Andreas Vesalius published *De Humani Corporis Fabrica*, the first complete study of human anatomy. Copernicus' simple diagram of a heliocentric solar system and Vesalius' detailed etchings of man's internal organs were staggering to medieval minds. In its way, Vesalius' anatomy was as shocking as Copernicus' description of a sun-centered cosmos; it violated the established belief in the body as the Temple of the Lord, home to spiritual heats and humors.

With these seminal works, Renaissance science simultaneously leaped out into space and began a detailed exploration into the mysteries of the human body. "I am not laboring to lay the foundation of any sect or doctrine, but of human utility and power," [228] Descartes declared.

In the late eighteenth and nineteenth centuries the abstract intellectual concepts thrown forth by the Scientific Revolution and the Enlightenment were subsumed by the material thump and hiss of steam engines, the roaring blasts of Bessemer steel furnaces, and the rolling hum of electrical dynamos - machines that embodied the brute force of the Industrial Revolution.

Since the triumph of the Industrial Revolution in the nineteenth century, it has become increasingly obvious that modern science and technology have ceased to be the civilizing vehicles their original innovators intended. In fact, some commentators see the techno-future our celeverness has contrived as driven by essentially barbaric impulses. "Today violence and aggression seem less sublimated than in previous periods of history," Herbert Marcuse commented, and our technological culture has come to "perpetuate and intensify the struggle for existence instead of alleviating it." [229] The moral neutrality of science, its freedom from the prison of imposed ends, has made it "impure, incapable or unwilling to refuse collaboration with the theoreticians and practitioners of legalized destruction and exploitation," herding us toward a world of "frightening absolutism."

Somewhere along the way we seem to have lost the original Hellenic notion that science is a means rather than an end; that, as Aristotle declared, "Every science and every inquiry... is thought to aim at some good." [230] Purists, such as Plato, actually disdained the practical application of scientific discoveries, and Archimedes ordered his famous machine to be destroyed after it had served its scientific purpose as a demonstration of the mathematics of specific gravity and leverage. The best Hellenic minds favored a search for the principles of "know-why" over the practicalities of "know-how," preferring to understand nature rather than rule it. Forgetting this old wisdom has landed us in the condition of frightening techno-absolutism we now inhabit.

\* \* \*

In our present unhappy context of ambiguity and alienation, of perhaps not being wanted at all, watching professional sporting events has replaced the real connections of a shattered sense of human community. Today, spectating the game has become a surrogate for the more tangible social interactions our techno-culture denies us. The teams we support supply us with an illusion of identity in a society that offers us few concrete ways to define ourselves; but even this transient shared experience is mostly spurious, since the players we lustily cheer on may have no local loyalty whatever, having been traded for a huge price from the other end of the country.

But for the hour or two that the game lasts, as we shout our throats raw for the Steelers, Leafs, or Yankees, we can pretend to share a common interest with the millions of other TV watchers drifting in the electronic wilderness. Since the glow of this brief communality is temporary and largely illusory, it has to shine a violent light to make its mark upon our starved social sensibilities.

And the high-priced players in modern body contact sports - our danger-prone stand-ins - know what's expected of them. Johnny Sample, ex-New York Jets lineman, describes the action vividly: "I came into him, elbows and knees flying. Now I could have jumped over him, touching him just enough to down the ball. But I didn't. And the result was that I broke three of his ribs." [231] Down in "The

Pit," where the two lines clash, "We're like a bunch of animals kicking and clawing and scratching at each other." In his book, *Violence Every Sunday*, football coach Mike Holovak said: "That's why people love it, it's a violent sport...the most violent sport man has invented." [232]

Sometimes spectators do cross the line between vicarious violence and the real thing. An anthropologist observing a battle between rival soccer fans on a British ferry noted that the club supporters were having a high old time. "They seemed to be enjoying themselves immensely, making a lot of noise, rushing dramatically up and down the stairs, spraying the firehoses everywhere, and throwing the occasional bottle or glass at the other side." [233] As they did so "they experienced a transcendent moment of community with their mates." Anthropologists describe such wild festivities as "deep play," an affirmation of tribal identity.

Less playfully, British soccer fans taunt their rivals with chants such as, "You're gonna get your fuckin' heads kicked in." Riots may erupt in the stadium, leading to injury and death. Even in the relative sanity of Holland fierce confrontations erupt between Amsterdam and Rotterdam teams, and the *ragazzi di stadio* of Italian clubs such as Juventus are notoriously aggressive. Ironically, American football, a far more bruising game than soccer, has provoked far fewer bloody stadium fights. Perhaps that is because the catharsis played out on the football field satisfies the spectators' need for release more graphically than the more skillful confrontations soccer provides.

The most personal of all violent body contact sports has to be the prizefight. Unlike the football player, protected by his padded uniform and backed by his team, boxers go alone and near naked into the ring. Their heads are unprotected by helmets, their chests and bellies are bare. Boxing is a bloody battle one-on-one, an elemental display with elementary rules in which two men hammer each other to the point of absolute pain and exhaustion. Recalling the fourteenth round in his final encounter with Smokin' Joe Frazier, in October 1975, Muhammad Ali said: "It was like death. The closest thing to dying that I know of." [234]

The bruising clash between two boxers or wrestlers inside the confines of a roped arena has become one of our few remaining "true" experiences in a treacherously ambiguous contemporary culture. Journalist Jeffrey T. Sammons remarked that "the sight of two sweaty gladiators standing tall in the ring, and the sound of glove against flesh all open a window to a simpler, more human-oriented past when muscle, might, and perhaps intelligence allowed us to control our own destiny." [235]

French cultural philosopher Roland Barthes lauded all-in wrestling as "the spectacle of excess," in which the spectators enjoy "the transient image of certain passions... (the) exaggeratedly visible explanation of Necessity." For Barthes, wrestling is a pantomime in which the fans experience tremendous pleasure watching the "moral mechanism" of suffering, justice, defeat and humiliation function in a pure form unobscured by the illusion of fair play. "Deprived of all resilience, the (defeated) wrestler's flesh is no longer anything but an unspeakable heap spread out on the floor, where it solicits relentless reviling and jubilation." What this fierce contest gives its audience, "is the euphoria of men raised for a while above the constitutive ambiguity of everyday situations," raising them to a realm "in which signs at last correspond to causes, without obstacle, without evasion, without contradiction."

What is absent from the prizefight or the melodramatic spectacle of all-in wrestling, however, is the element of true and final danger present in the bullfight. Unlike the matador, a boxer or wrestler never knowingly offers up his life; but a momentary error of judgment or lapse of concentration can cripple or kill a bullfighter, unless his nerves are screwed to the very highest pitch of awareness. Despite the fact that the bull's bloody end is almost always certain, the danger is real, and death can come to the bullfighter, too, in a public climax that is also an intensely personal moment. At five in the afternoon, Lorca intoned in his vivid lament for the matador, Ignacio Sanchez Mejias, the bull is bellowing, the crowd is howling, while the dying man's "wounds were burning like suns." [236]

In so many movies and TV series it is an act of violence which marks the truly personal moment. The cowboy anti-heroes of Sam Peckinpah's movie, *The Wild Bunch*, for example, come most fully and unambiguously alive only in the instant in which they quixotically take on an entire Mexican army, and die in a bloody hail of gunfire. In *The Wild Bunch*, as in many of the finest Westerns, the action is played out in an emotional and spiritual desert where language fails and guns speak.

In this bleak and simple landscape of the soul, hero and outlaw are two sides of the same coin, and violence is the only way to assert the human presence in an existential blankness. When bullets fly and blood spurts, all ambiguities are abolished, all doubts are murdered and the clear white light of mythical truth comes shining through the gunfire. In Peckinpah's terse phrase, "violence cuts the crap." [237]

The figure of the lone sheriff or gunfighter confronting his opponent or opponents gun in hand is a prime American image. Or there is the outlaw, even the gangster, shooting it out with the law in a hail of lead. It's Billy the Kid, Gary Cooper in *High Noon*, Bonnie and Clyde, Jessie James, mafiosi "goodfellas," Dirty Harry, the righteously murderous cop, and the rape-provoked female killers in *Thelma and Louise*. In *Butch Cassidy and the Sundance Kid* the criminal pair become tragic heroes in the fury of the final shoot-out. The lone hero-villain may perish in the gunfire, like Sterling Hayden's mortally wounded trigger man in *The Asphalt Jungle*, or James Cagney's many streetwise, punk-knight personas, but the ultimate violence always defines the ultimate intimacy.

It might be said that violence is the defining American mode. Where an Englishman or a Hindu might be defined by his class or caste, a Spaniard by the force of his national history, an Irishman by his shared national tragedy, Americans - a nation of displaced persons seeking equality of opportunity - have little in common except their personal or inherited rejection of an original homeland. Social factors are too confused and particular to provide an American with his or her ultimate identity in a fluid society that prides itself on its social and economic mobility, its freedom to constantly reinvent one's personality and one's fate.

However, the international appeal of bloody action movies, whether imported from the U.S. or homemade, reveals that the appetite for violence as self-definition has become as as the abstract, techno-culture that manufactures them. As the world's economy is globalized, the vicarious violence of films and TV has become a universal language of shared images. In Bombay or Berlin, Tokyo or Toledo, Nairobi or Nimes, *The Wild Bunch* provides the individual viewer with the thrill that comes from knowing that, despite everything in his life that diminishes him, he can dream of a power to cut the crap.

This hunger for violence, both surrogate and actual, has become a common phenomenon, but it is especially prevalent in America.

The United States produces most of the "entertainments" popular in our time, and Americans are killed or wounded by their fellow citizens at a far higher rate than Englishmen, Germans or Japanese. It seems that, in the bloodstream of one of the most technologically developed societies in the world, there beats a furiously primitive pulse.

However, although the daily level of violence in America is considerably higher than, say Europe's, the U.S. has had far fewer of the bloody convulsions on its own territory that, over the centuries, have killed and injured tens of millions of Europeans. Only the American Civil War can begin to match the wholesale level of home-grown European slaughter; but even the casualties in that conflict pale before the mountains of corpses left by the two World Wars in Europe in this century alone. It might be that, while Europe interrupts its episodes of peace with orgies of bloodletting, in the U.S. the pulse of violence beats more evenly, and far more modestly.

If Americans tend to settle their grievances with one another, and with the larger society, more violently than many other people, it may be that such ferocities are an American-style gut revulsion against a modern world that seems to have surrendered all too easily to an inhuman regimen of social and economic abstraction. Where the disciplined Japanese crowd into sardine-can commuter trains to go to work, and labor endless hours without a murmur of protest; where the Germans, haunted by their recent past, have made their "economic miracle" into a religion of conformity; where the huddled masses of Hong Kong are happy to have any work at any wage, many Americans seem less able to squeeze their souls into the straitjacket of the post-industrial processes that rule the modern world. In America, particularly, violence is a directly physical and emotional reaction against the slippery abstractions of modern life.

Americans, it seems to me, have the liveliest sense of this balance than any other developed nation. They appear to be least able to tolerate too much distortion between private truth and public lies. Their sense of this balance is the essence of U.S. democracy. When that sense of balance gets badly out of whack Americans often react violently, out of an instinct of preservation for their basic and vital human truths. Or, as Octavio Paz shrewdly remarked: "Would it be true to say that North Americans prefer to use reality rather than to know it?" [238]

However that is, America's turbulent pulse has provoked many

109

social crises in our time, from Detroit, Harlem, Newark and Watts in the 1960s to the citywide Los Angeles riots and arson of 1992, on to the bruising confrontations between protesters and police at the World Trade Organization meeting in Seattle in late 1999. In Detroit, the urban tension has been so drastic that the heart of the city is now a wasteland where corn is grown on burned-out lots, under the shadow of proud glass commercial towers - conjuring up the image of an imminent return to a preindustrial agrarian culture.

Take that icon of turbulence in our time, the inner-city "gangbanger," whose rebellious responses are manifest in his gross tattoos, baggy clothes, colored bandanas, harsh rap lyrics and wild use of firearms. The ruling wisdom concerning urban gang members in any society - true as far as it goes - is that they suffer from limited economic opportunity compounded by a breakdown in the traditional family. Others regard gang life as essentially pathological, a cancer on society, for which we cannot seem to find a cure.

But if we drop the condescending role of being doctors to diseased patients, we may find that the gangbanger has something to tell us, something we need to know. We might perceive that his life experience is a crude, unfocused expression of protest against the brutalities of our economic system, a troubled pool reflecting the polluted landscape that surrounds it, unclouded by polite pretence.

Perhaps, too, gang life is one of the few arenas left in our over-abstracted culture in which the primal energies of violence find open expression, not for spectators but for participants. A gang member may not be able to articulate these feelings, but that does not mean he cannot know them in his bones.

Erich Fromm suggested that destructive and self-destructive human beings are a fascinating paradox: "they express life *turning against itself in the striving to make sense of it.*" [239] (Fromm's italics.) Herbert Marcuse goes further, pointing out that violence is "an integral part of culture, so that the attainment or approximation of the cultural goals takes place *through* the practice of cruelty and violence." [240] While mainstream society tries to pretend this isn't so, gang culture openly lives out these hard facts.

The gang life of places like South-Central Los Angeles, Harlem, Detroit, and a host of other American and European cities is a raw reflection of the intense pressures built into society at large - those brutal economic and cultural imperatives we accept as inescapable and try not to think about as we struggle through the day. We are

shocked by the raw rampages of inner-city gang life yet fail to perceive that nowadays the most powerful and pervasive kind of disturbance springs from the strategies of the global economy in which
we all have to fight for our survival. In a sense, the gangs are our
own homegrown *intifada* - a spontaneous revolt against the far more
profoundly oppressive hidden forces at play in the social mainstream. George Soros, a leading capitalist, suggests that there is "an
ongoing conflict between market values and other, more traditional
value systems, which has aroused strong passions and
antagonisms." [241]
　　The stress that most directly and painfully impacts us every day
is derived from an economic system that drives large segments of
our fellow citizens to the wall. "I used to have control over my life,"
said a working mother, quoted in *Time* magazine during the run-
up to the 1996 presidential election. "Now I could scream and cry
and have a nervous breakdown." [242] This cri-de-coeur reveals that
she, like the rest of us, exists in a world which moves with ruthless
speed to maximize every advantage, no matter who suffers, no
matter how many of us feel exhausted, alienated, and overwhelmed.

　　I began to really understand something about this early in the
morning of May 1, 1992, two days after Los Angeles was disrupted
by the explosion of arson, looting and shooting that would eventually claim more than fifty lives and destroy hundreds of buildings.
I drove up to the heights of Mulholland Drive to get a panoramic
overview of the extraordinary tumult tearing at the city. The fires
had come within a few blocks of my house on a quiet Hollywood
street, the smell of burning polluted the air of my garden, but I had
no clear grasp of what was happening in the city at large, apart
from the hectic images projected on television.
　　On this bright spring Friday morning pillars of smoke hung
in the sunshine, rising to mingle with L.A.'s usual smoggy inver-
sion layer. Seen from my high vantage point, the core of the vast
Los Angeles Basin appeared to have imploded, as if a volcano had
blown its top. Up where I was standing mockingbirds trilled their
dawn songs; down below, however, the city seemed to have suffered a human seismic event more shaking to the spirit than any
earthquake.
　　This image of a human quake stayed with me in the weeks and
months following the "riot" or "rebellion," as it was variously

named. I read the endless editorials analyzing the reasons for the unrest, listened to the many pundits pontificate, heard innumerable officials obfuscate, and was left with a feeling that something crucial was absent in all these explanations.

What they missed was any sense of the April upheaval as an act of violence *in its own right*. Anger over the acquittal of four police officers charged with beating a black motorist may have sparked the explosion, but the faces of the burners and the looters, brazenly exposed on TV screens, registered a kind of fierce delight as they torched buildings and helped themselves to a selective array of goodies, from VCRs and camcorders to disposable diapers. In some respects, it seemed to me, the riot was an impromptu, unauthorized reversion to the rituals of a Roman Saturnalia or the medieval merrymaking presided over by the Lord of Misrule, in which the lower social orders temporarily turn the established hierarchy on its head and expose its unacknowledged hypocrises.

\*   \*   \*

Violence of feeling, thought, and action is a very human urge to touch something real in a welter of intangibles. Of course, many of these intangibles consist of the compromises built into the texture of any functioning society: the necessary humbug of civilization without which our lives would indeed be nasty, brutish and short.

The question is: how much humbug should any man or woman reasonably accept? Too little makes it difficult for any social system to function. Too much can fatally diminish an individual's sense of himself.

However one views it, the vast public appetite for violence - mostly proxy violence - might be regarded as one of the last expressions of our humanity under the forward charge of the technical phenomenon. Having more or less subdued the earth, as Jehovah commanded, mankind has come close to losing any living sense of its intrinsic self. In our often soul-sickening world of abstractions and ambiguities, violence provides a passionate pathway connecting us with certain basic truths about the human condition. In this life-affirming sense, it offers us a kind of ugliness clothing a terrible beauty.

It is vital to grasp this perception, given that our victory in the long war against nature has come to threaten our individual and collective freedom, our very sense of ourselves as human beings. Ceasing to be the instrument of liberation conceived by the innovators and inventors of the scientific and industrial revolutions, our cleverness has bound us into an iron cage whose bars might be even more difficult to loosen than the old bonds of nature.

In truth, our next great struggle will have to be waged against the very weapons we fashioned in our original fight with the forces that ruled humanity's fate for thousands of years. Hobbes's comment that "There is no such thing as perpetual tranquility of mind while we live here, because life itself is but motion and can never be without desire, or without fear, no more than without sense," [243] has taken on a new and ever more anxious meaning. Hobbes added that there could be no contentment but in proceeding, though one might say that the lesson of the contemporary world is that there is also precious little contentment in proceeding.

The Iraqui farmer in Hassuna, watching the high-tech warplanes buzzing his ancient fields, might not be surprised that, after so much effort and ingenuity, we have only succeeded in replacing one servitude with another. However, an optimist must believe that the coming war of man with his own world-mastering technologies will generate yet another fascinating dimension of human reality.

# 7
# dangerous loving

All personal human experience begins in the family. This fact holds true whether we are American, Asian or African, live in nuclear families with one or two parents and siblings, or in extended families with grandparents, parents, aunts, uncles and cousins. Even children raised in orphanages, or in collective organizations such as Israeli kibbutzim, experience a sense of family with those who shape and share their childhood experience. For better or worse, the family in all its forms communicates to the child its fundamental sense of worth or worthlessness.

Despite a great deal of evidence to the contrary, our fond mythology of the family clings to the belief that it is a cradle of love and safety in a complex and confusing world. But in reality the family is an emotional pressure cooker steaming with raw feelings, a cauldron of dangerous loving whose heat forever forges our characters.

The sense of being cooked in a family's emotional crucible begins at birth. If the infant is a first child, he will likely suffer the fallout from his parents' unresolved emotional problems; problems made all the more painful by a rude shift from coupledom to parenthood. If there are older children, there will be a contest for a place in the warmth of parental regard, and for status in the sibling hierarchy. At the same time the child's nerves experience the pressure of his own urgent self-explorations, and the counter-pressure of his need to attract adult care and affection. One way or another, a baby soon begins to be the repository of all the family's social and personal fears and confusions, plus all the unconscious guilts and internalized repressions handed down through generations.

In the midst of these stresses, a child learns early on that violence is integral to the human condition. In fact, he discovers this at birth, for the very act of being born is certainly one of the most turbulent psychic and physical shocks any person ever suffers.

Impelled by the convulsive muscular spasms of the mother's womb, the fetus is squeezed through the vaginal sheath like toothpaste through a tube. Flexible soft bones in the skull and torso bend forcibly under the immense strain of the birth canal, until the fetus, abruptly metamorphosed into a "baby," bursts through the tight, distended vulva into the alien air. The first cry, activating the dormant air bag in its chest, is an echo of the eons its took for gills to evolve into amphibian lungs. Still connected to the placenta by the umbilicus, the newborn is laid upon its mother's breast. It senses the maternal heartbeat, a sound familiar from the womb, yet somehow different: comforting yet strange, the drumbeat of desire.

A newborn child takes the world into himself through other people. He begins to learn hard lessons about the difference between inside and outside, me and not-me. He is taught to distinguish good from bad, the naughty from the nice, the clean from the dirty, what is acceptable from what's not. He learns that food goes from outside to inside, and shit completes the circle. He discovers that, for reasons tough to fathom, food is okay in the mouth but not slung across the table, and shit is okay in the potty but not on the floor.

Along with the loving feelings associated with birth and mothering, there is also a strong element of antagonism inherent in the relationship of a mother and her infant. French "anti-psychiatrists" Gilles Deleuze and Felix Guattari call the baby a "desiring-machine" that "breathes...heats...eats...shits and fucks." [244] Psychologist Hanna Segal, a disciple of Melanie Klein, suggests that "A hungry, raging infant, screaming and kicking, phantasies that he is actually attacking the breast, tearing and destroying it, and experiences his own screams which tear him and hurt him as the torn breast attacking him in his own inside." [245] The child feels that her mother is "the primal persecutor," [246] Klein asserted, attacking the child's body, engendering terrifying anxieties.

For an infant, the first year of family life offers basic, often searing discoveries of the varieties of pain and pleasure. Watching his parents' faces for every small sign of approval or disapproval, he soon discovers they can smile wonderfully or scowl horribly. And the voices that chatter away at him as he lies helpless on his back can coo or curse, comfort or condemn, laying down the basic pattern of all his future human interactions. All that a newborn has to arm him in his fight for a place in the family nest is the violence of his feelings, expressed in forceful howls of desire or distress.

In a poignant footnote in *The Anatomy of Human Destructiveness*, Erich Fromm pointed out that infants pour their furious energies into the language of their cries and the vehemence of their reactions. "Since they are powerless, they have to use their own methods, those of guerrilla warfare, as it were," [247] he wrote. In the instinctual fight for the right to be themselves, they protest their condition of powerlessness by pushing away the feeding spoon, by often deliberately dirtying their diapers, and by disturbing the parental sleep as frequently as they can with the vehemence of their shrieking - those raw, despairing wails that shred a mother's or a father's nerves.

Tennyson put it this way, in the prologue to In Memoriam:

> *But what am I?*
> *An infant crying in the night:*
> *An infant crying for the light:*
> *And with no language but a cry.* [248]

One way or another, adults use force and the threat of force as an agent of control, and children soon learn that certain kinds of violence are sanctioned social strategies. In effect, adults behave like any elite whose power is challenged. "They use physical force, often tempered with bribery, to protect their position," [249] Fromm noted. Parents may handle an infant brusquely, or try to seduce him with extra milk, or intimidate him with rough voices. "No mercy is shown in this war until victory is achieved," Fromm commented. Consequently, adults of every social class and condition have, as infants, shared "the common experience of having once been powerless and of having fought for their freedom." Or, as radical psychiatrist R.D. Laing put it: "The baby is subjected to forces of outrageous violence, called love." [250]

The notion that families are defined as much by fierce conflict as warm affection is both a radical and an ancient view. It is radical in the way in which it "challenges a viewpoint which labels violence, abrupt change, tension and struggles between subordinate and superordinate individuals as deviant or abnormal situations." [251] Family life includes the experience of "bitter feelings, anger, hatred, much physical punishment of children, pokes and slaps of husbands and wives, and not altogether pitched battles between family members." [252] To this catalogue of conflict one can add the sexual and emotional abuse of children by parents, of wives by husbands, of husbands by wives.

As children, we soon discover that violence in various direct or subtle forms is crucial to the process known as "growing up" - an often painful experience in which each individual becomes a member of his particular family, social circle, and the human family at large. The emotional conflict a child experiences may be covert or overt, hidden under the cloak of loving concern or nakedly revealed, but one way or another it is fundamental to his becoming a social being in any society. The force of others' feelings and his own, played out in daily life and in dreams, creates his personality and determines his place in the world.

Some children react fiercely to this hard conditioning, others helplessly inherit the pain of generations. Describing a schizophrenic, Laing wrote that the body of the boy, Paul, was "a haunted graveyard in which the ghosts of several generations still walked, while their physical remains rotted away." [253] The boy's family, Laing observed, "had buried their dead *in each other.*" (Laing's italics.) [254]

The brute fact is that, to become members of the human community, we are all condemned to do violence to our innate selves, to a greater or lesser degree. This is the process called "socialization." "Man is up against himself," wrote anthropologist Ralph L. Holloway Jr. "He is up against social structure - he is up against culture," he said, echoing Freud's thesis in *Civilization and Its Discontents.* "These are his costs as well as his gains. The structures, social and symbolic, which permits his adaptations and the execution of shared tasks to insure his existence, also insure frustration, pain and conflict." [255] The primary battleground of this radical conflict is the family.

*   *   *

Apart from the home scenario, the hard game of socialization-through-violence continues in kindergarten and on the playground. You can observe this when the under-fives are let out to play in the schoolyard and the teacher relaxes her control over the group.

At first the bunch of small bodies around the climbing frame seems like one collective animal, with more arms and legs than a demented centipede; but in the fierce pushing and shoving the various personalities are defined. There may be howls and tears, but mostly the kids end up in a pile of flailing limbs at the foot of the slide, kicking and shouting. The teacher knows that such "friendly" fights seldom degenerate into vicious battles, but all the same they are a tough test of each child's mettle.

I remember watching my four-year-old son's painful struggle to claim his place in the society of children his own age. Looking down from the fifth floor window of our apartment, I followed Paul's social initiation as if it were happening in a live video game, an almost abstract pattern of behavior in which the boy and his peers were colored dots bouncing off one another.

The focus of the action was a wooden jungle-gym and slide on the communal green behind our building, reserved for the under-fives. On his first day on the green, Paul appeared on the edge of my field of view, a bright spot in his crimson sweater. He paused there, well outside the circle of the kids around the climbing frame, nervous and hesitating.

A bright boy and very open, Paul was easily hurt. He made several tentative moves to penetrate the climbing-frame cluster, but each time his own timidity betrayed him and he fell back. Suffering with him, I sensed the hammering of his heart, the shame of his rejection, his intense yearning to be one of the gang. Screwing up his courage, Paul again approached the circle, and was repulsed several more times. The other kids, sensing his vulnerability, gave him a particularly hard time as the price of his ticket of entry into their tight little community.

For a while it seemed Paul would never make it. The invisible membrane that enclosed the group resisted Paul's shy attempts to poke through. Even at my elevated distance I could see his resolve weaken, his approaches become progressively less assured each time he was repelled, until he finally seemed at the point of retreating. But I'm sure he knew in his gut that if his courage failed, he might never be accepted in the jungle-gym crowd.

A surprising act of violence saved him. Just as Paul was about to slink away, one bright yellow speck broke off from the bunch and deliberately banged into him, knocking him flat on his back. In an instant Paul was reduced from a distinct spot to a smudged crimson blob.

Up in my eyrie, I held my breath. Would my son bolt or stand his ground? Would the attack wipe him out or stiffen his spine? The assault was an opportunity as well as a challenge, and Paul could use it or be crushed.

He used it. After being knocked on his ass, Paul jumped up, confronted his attacker, and pushed back, hard. I trembled for him in that instant, knowing how he must be shaking, expecting a fist in his face. But Paul held his ground, nose-to-nose with Yellow Dot, swapping glare for glare, aware that any show of weakness in that instant would forever ban him from the gang.

For one long, heart-stopping instant, everything hung in the balance.

Finally, Yellow Dot turned curtly on his heel, and Paul followed the path he opened into the group around the climbing frame. The invisible membrane closed behind him and he was inside. As the kids raced round and round the slide I lost sight of his red sweater in the happy blur of color.

Even seen in the abstract, the process was as brutal as it was necessary; Paul had to earn his place in that small world. The boy who knocked him down had tried his pluck. Paul passed the test and was welcomed into the community. His daring act of counter-violence had earned him a place on the green, and on later occasions I saw him handle newcomers just as roughly.

But a child's trial by violence is not limited to the world out there. Within each child is also a creative-destructive universe of turbulent sensibilities and symbols, that must be mastered.

On the night of his first acceptance into the group on the communal green, Paul was attacked by bad dreams. He sweated profusely, bashed his pillow in sleep, peed in his bed. Disturbed by his sobs, I staggered half-asleep to his bedroom and hugged him until he quietened. Holding the boy, the images of my own childhood dream-terrors flashed one upon the other. Adults often forget this state of primal fright, this naked experience of psychic fear children know all too well.

Dreams and nightmares are as real to a child as any daytime occurrence, for there is no membrane to sheath the young soul, no clear division between what is happening in internally and externally. As the Swiss child psychologist Jean Piaget pointed out, it is only around seven years of age that a child begins to grasp that mental imagery is something that happens in his head. Before that age children perceive every action and event as symbolic; "and it is when symbolism is declining and when true concepts are taking the place of imagined preconcepts, that thought leads to an awareness sufficient to allow of relative, internal localization." [256] What the learned Swiss was saying, in his typically convoluted fashion, is that very young children "think" solely in terms of charged images, leaving their minds unprotected by such organizing notions as Me and Not-Me, Waking and Dreaming. "Even in imaginative daydreaming and in dreams themselves, the imitation of experienced situations and of people and things, often strikingly exact even to the minutest detail, is translated purely into images," [257] Piaget wrote. For children, Kant's observation that perceptions without conceptions are blind is particularly apt.

\* \* \*

The role of violence in shaping the human spirit is vividly apparent in fairy tales and nursery rhymes. The stories which generations of children have adored are charged with all manner of turmoil, chaos and atrocity, of the most extreme variety. If you spend an afternoon in the children's section of any public library riffling through books of fairy tales you will discover a world ripe with a tonic barbarity.

In many of these stories human and animal characters are flayed, buried alive, and scalded. They have their throats slit, their bodies dismembered, their mouths stuffed with red-hot embers. They're thrust into ovens, into vats of boiling water, into tubs of bubbling pitch. Parents abandon their luckless offspring in burning deserts and raging blizzards, eat them alive and dead, raw or cooked, commit incest with them, poison them, tear out their hearts, their tongues, their nails, and gouge out their eyes. Hills open up and swallow children whole. Horned witches make cakes with blood drawn from sleeping families. Monstrous spiders, sea monsters, werewolves, ghosts and goblins leap out from every page.

Yet children appear to have an insatiable relish for such terrifying delights. They often seem to want the very worst to happen. British psychoanalyst Anthony Storr recalled a graphic instance of this appetite in one five-year-old girl. When read a story about a boy who is rescued at the last moment before being thrown into a cask of bubbling pitch, she protested: "But I *want* him to be thrown into the pitch!" [258]

Fairy stories, like the folk tales from which they originate, are apprehensions of the fact and force of violence, transformed by the imagination. Like any act of art, the tales reimagine our feelings and our intuitions, translating them into narratives the mind and heart can integrate into the scheme of experience. Maurice Sendak, one of the most popular children's authors and illustrators of modern times, portrayed the hairy monsters who bedevil the hero Max in *Where the Wild Things Are* as foul of breath, sporting bristling nose hair and bloodshot eyes. "That's how they looked to me when I was a kid," Sendak said. [259]

In an essay on fairy tales, writer Aviva Layton commented that "Children's inner fantasy lives, like our own, are rampant with sexuality and aggression. Creative violence provides an imaginative embodiment of those fears and tensions, a channel through which subconscious desires can find relief." [260] Children are drawn to images of cannibalism, Layton suggested, because they have the experience of being "eaten up many times in the course of a day - by a smothering mother, an oppressive teacher, an insensitive father or a rival sibling - and it's folly to assume that the little darlings aren't itching to return the favor. It is the aesthetic embodiment of these secret and unacceptable fantasies [in fairy tales] which enables the child to free himself from them." [261]

Traditional fairy story characters often have to trip their way through thickets of fright, struggling to survive violations and mutilations. In the Brothers Grimm's tale, *The Maiden Without Hands*, for instance, a miller's daughter's hands are cut off by her "loving" father, in fulfillment of a Faustian bargain with the devil. With her maimed arms bound behind her back, the nameless girl sets out to wander the world. Though she meets and marries a king who fits her with silver hands, the mutilated maiden is threatened with the loss of her eyes and tongue before the tale's happy ending. [262]

The British novelist Angela Carter, who discovered a richly ironic vein of allegory in fairy tales, took up the history of the abused and innocent maiden featured in many traditional tales. In *The Bloody Chamber*, a fable for adults, Carter's heroine travels to the honeymoon castle of her legendary Marquis. The Marquis, described by the girl as dark and leonine with eyes marked by an "absolute absence of light," takes his little Marquise "into marriage, into exile." [263]

The girl is deflowered, impaled by her demon lover's lust. "I clung to him as though only the one who had inflicted the pain could comfort me for suffering it." [264] She learns that the Marquis, a descendant of Dracula, has a secret torture chamber in his castle, complete with a terrible Iron Maiden - a metal casket shaped like a woman and filled with spikes. She discovers, in short, that she is destined to die as the ultimate sacrifice of "love." At the last moment, however, she is saved by a kind of maternal telepathy, that summons her mother to her rescue. Her mother shoots the old pervert dead, and the girl returns to the everyday world, indelibly marked by shame.

In Carter's version, innocence connives at its own victimization. The heroine in *The Bloody Chamber* learns a shocking lesson in the toils of the "tender, delicious ecstasy of excitement" [265] of her honeymoon with Dracula's scion. The girl becomes a woman in this learning, while her brave mother, "eagle-featured, indomitable," [266] saves her from her folly.

But not all mothers are so benign in fairy tales and nursery rhymes. A British lullaby popular in the Napoleonic Wars of the early nineteenth century has a mother singing to her naughty, squalling infant that Bonaparte will tear him limb from limb, "just as pussy tears a mouse:"

*And he'll beat you, beat you, beat you,*
*And he'll beat you all to pap,*
*And he'll eat you, eat you, eat you,*
*Every morsel, snap, snap, snap.* [267]

Folk ballads, from which most nursery rhymes derive, include many such violent maternal figures. In the old Scottish ballad, *The Cruel Mother*, a woman curses her newborn, stabs it with a penknife, and "howket a grave by the light o' the moon," [268] to bury her sweet babe in. "Smile na sae sweet, my bonie babe," she croons over her infant's grave, "And ye smile sae sweet, ye'll smile me dead." [269] The child survives, returns her mother's curse, and consigns the woman to hell.

The notion that a mother, upon whom a helpless babe relies for sustenance and affection, could also kill haunts many a child's nightmares. Mothers who nourish and succor a child can also threaten its life, through malice, neglect or ignorance, and the child senses this possibility from an early age. Totally beholden to maternal power, a child feels its vulnerability intensely, especially at those moments when, exhausted and rattled by the relentless demands of parenting, the mother exhibits a fierce scowl and maybe handles her offspring roughly.

According to Jung, the figure of the Terrible Mother represents "anything secret, hidden, dark; the abyss, the world of the dead, anything that devours, seduces, and poisons, that is terrifying and inescapable like fate." [270] In other words, the Terrible Mother is the obverse of maternal solicitude and sympathy, of "all that is benign, all that cherishes and sustains." [271]

To soften the apprehension of a motherhood capable of such frightening things, fairy tales and folklore often disguise the cruel mother figure as a stepmother. Snow White's stepmother, jealous of her beauty, sends her out into the forest to be killed. "Bring me back Snow White's lungs and liver as proof," [272] the stepmother tells the huntsman she has chosen for this evil deed. The man takes pity on the pretty girl, kills a boar in her place, and offers the animal's organs to the stepmother, who boils them up and eats them. Snow White, after finding refuge with the Seven Dwarfs, is hounded by her stepmother, who slips her a deadly apple.

When the prince wakens her from her poisoned trance, Snow White's joyful triumph over her wicked stepmother is spiced by a cruel and malicious delight. Forced to put on red-hot slippers heated in a fire, the evil woman dances till she falls down dead.

Anne Sexton renders the stepmother's dance of death in her poem, *Snow White and the Seven Dwarfs*, but with a twist. The poet implies that Snow White and her stepmother share the same fatal female urge to turn to the mirror and ask the obsessive question: "Who is the fairest of them all?"

> *And so she danced until she was dead,*
> *a subterranean figure,*
> *her tongue flicking in and out*
> *like a gas jet.*
> *Meanwhile Snow White held court,*

123

*rolling her china-blue doll eyes open and shut*
*and sometimes referring to her mirroR*
*as women do.* [273]

In *The Uses of Enchantment,* Bruno Bettleheim quoted Friedrich Schiller's comment that "Deeper meaning resides in the fairy tales told to me in my childhood than in the truth that is taught by life." [274] Bettleheim declared that a child must be helped to make sense of the turmoil of his feelings, for a child "needs ideas on how to bring his inner house into order, and on that basis be able to create order in his life." [275] Children require a moral education which teaches "not through abstract ethical concepts but through that which seems tangibly right and therefore meaningful to him." [276] The terrifying delights of fairy tales echo the intensities of a child's struggle to bring his inner house into order.

However, some intensely imaginative adults never achieve such order; their inherited childhood universe remains forever under threat. Speaking of his wife, Sylvia Plath, the poet Ted Hughes said that adult horrors "were merely the open wounds in her idea of the great civilized crime of intelligence." [277] Plath's reactions to hurts in other people and animals, and even tiny desecrations of plant life were extremely fierce, Hughes remarked. R.D. Laing could be speaking of Plath when he wrote that "The Dreamer who dreams our dreams knows far more of us than we know of it. The mind of which we are unaware is aware of us. It is we who are out of our minds." [278]

At Kingsley Hall, the London haven for troubled souls Laing established with his colleague David Cooper, patients were encouraged to regress to a state of blissful infantilism. They were free to smear shit on the walls, scream at the doctors, and generally break down the role structure of the conventional mental hospital. Laing lived in Kingsley Hall for a year, and, in the unkempt manner of his dress, was frequently taken for a patient by visitors. In this milieu patients cured doctors as much as doctors cured patients, and the naked emotional violence of such a mutually therapeutic experience enriched both parties, Laing asserted.

In *Madness and Civilization,* Michel Foucault described the vulnerability to such naked emotional turmoil as "the sovereign enterprise of unreason." [279] Jacques Lacan and his followers claim that for schizophrenics and other "madmen," madness is a richer kind of communication, a creative violence done to the Cartesian formulations of "I think therefore I am." In Laing and Lacan's view, schizophrenics deal in a fragmented communication that more truly reflects the split soul of modern man and his "divided self." For anti-psychiatrists such as Laing and Lacan, Freud's gloomy description of civilization and its discontents is not an irremediable state of the human condition but a condemnation of modern life. They regard repression as a rape of the psyche rather than a necessary sublimation. For them, true desire is warped and twisted by the overarching culture, and furious means, even madness, may be necessary to create new freedoms.

In their essence, such notions are essentially metaphysical. Job's old cry, "What is man that thou shouldest visit him every morning, and try him every moment?" echoes in the depths of every psychological therapy, every sociological concept, every anthropological construct. The human pain remains, but the answer is still absent.

*   *   *

In the secular West, as in most "advanced" societies, we no longer see life as a numinous event charged with critical transitions between one state of being and another. For instance, we seldom celebrate the momentous change every human being experiences as he grows into adulthood, emerging out of the rich yet often terrifying state of consciousness we call childhood. In this transition the child in a young person "dies" so that an adult may be born.

This symbolic experience is blunted or ignored in the so-called developed societies. The rituals of the contemporary youth culture, while rampant and uproarious, lack real resonance. Pubertal rites of passage are only grudgingly acknowledged by the mainstream adult society, and mostly a young person is left alone to find a purely personal path through the thickets of confusion. Apart from some now largely vestigial rituals, such as the Catholic confirmation and the Jewish barmitzvah, the West is bereft of meaningful ceremonies of pubertal transition.

Less "developed" societies are often far wiser in this respect. One of the most extraordinary and powerful ceremonies of pubertal transition, for example, is to be found among the remote Orokaiva peoples of Papua New Guinea. When Orokaivan boys and girls are initiated into adulthood, they go through a graphic transformation from "prey" into "hunter." Beginning as a kind of human prey, pursued by adults wearing terrifying masks made of tropical bird plumage topped by pig's tusks, the children are metamorphosed into grown men and women in a rigorous ritual.

Covered in a huge cape that blinds them, the children are led out of the village to a hut deep in the forest. In this hut they cannot eat normal food, can't wash, speak aloud or see out. Subjected to a process that mimics death, the half-starved kids are told that they have become ancestral ghosts.

Symbolically deceased, the initiates become spiritualized, reports French anthropologist Andre Iteanu. As spirits, they are put through tests and ordeals, taught special dances, and become confidants of secrets only adults know. They are given feathered masks as symbols of their initiation, and play flutes and bull roarers, just as spirits do. From having been prey, the children become hunters who strut and dance, charged with an adult power.

To characterize the fecund energies present in such ceremonies, anthropologist Maurice Bloch coined the phrase "rebounding violence." [280] In Bloch's view, rebounding violence describes a kind of life-reversal in which a person is symbolically "killed," to negate his or her earthly birth and childhood. "Thus, by leaving this life, it is possible to see oneself and others as part of something permanent, therefore life-transcending," [281] Bloch declared. He suggested that this ritual death, followed by a "dramatic violence of the return to the mundane," [282] explained the fierce symbolisms present in so many religious phenomena.

In our modern unritualized cultures, experiences similar to Bloch's account of "rebounding violence" still occur in the transitions of puberty, but without meaningful ceremony. Young men and women experiment with sex, drugs and alcohol, or achieve a spasm of private ecstasy in the public mania of a rock concert. The effects of such unritualized events can be devastating or liberating, according to the individual temperament and imagination, but they seldom provide the integrated ceremonial transition into adulthood enjoyed by young Orokaivans. Yet one way or another, our adolescents also experience the demise of childhood as a kind of "death" - an emotionally turbulent experience that can be almost as traumatic as being born.

While many adolescents may become neurotic, and some may end up delinquent or even psychotic, others, "although deviating dangerously... eventually come to contribute an original bit to an emerging style of life," [283] according to psychologist Erik Erikson. "The very danger which they have sensed has forced them to mobilize capacities to see and say, to dream and plan, to design and construct new ways."

The French erotophile, Georges Bataille, captured the agitated condition of an adolescent's private initiation into adult sexuality in his short autobiographical novel, *Story of the Eye*. Bataille, then sixteen, watches young Simone dip her naked buttocks and vulva in a saucer of milk meant for the cat. Simone, Bataille recounted, "so bluntly craved any upheaval that the faintest call from the senses gave her a look directly suggestive of all things linked to deep sexuality, such as blood, suffocation, sudden terror, crime." [284] According to Bataille, "Violence alone, blind violence, can burst the barriers of the rational world and lead us into continuity." [285]

Famous instances of wholly personal, perilous, yet ultimately liberating adolescent second-birth experiences come from the history of temperaments as varied as William James and Carl Gustav Jung. James, considered the father of American psychology, brother to novelist Henry James, rescued himself from a prolonged domination by his father by provoking a spiritual collapse.

Henry James Sr. openly relished his hold on his famous sons. He described this domination as "a firm grip upon the coat tails of my Willy and my Harry, who both vituperate me beyond measure because I won't let them go." [286] William James was bullied by his parent into switching from the study of painting, which he loved, to the sciences, that he struggled to master. Under such stress, James responded with a frenzied nervous crisis, followed by a religious experience that changed his life.

"Suddenly there fell upon me without any warning, just as if it came out of the darkness, a horrible fear of my own existence," [287] James remembered. He had a vision of himself as an epileptic he had seen in an asylum; a black-haired youth with greenish skin, sitting with his knees drawn up to his chin like a sort of sculptured Egyptian cat or Peruvian mummy. "That shape am I," James thought. "Something hitherto solid within my breast gave way entirely, and I became a mass of quivering fear. After this the universe was changed for me altogether." [288] In the force of this horror, James discovered his own kind of God, the deity who answered his gut cry for help. The psychologist's glimpse into the abyss advanced his liberation from the grip his father had on his spirit.

Something similar happened to Jung. In his auto-biographical memoir, *Memories, Dreams, Reflections*, Jung wrote of a terrible dream that changed his life.

In his twelfth year the young Carl Gustav, the dutiful son of a strict Lutheran pastor, dreamed of God. God sat on his golden throne, high above the roof of Basle cathedral, whose new, brightly glazed tiles sparkled in the sun. The boy, tossing and turning in fitful sleep, was tormented by this idyllic vision. "What does God want?" he cried out in his dream. "I must find out what God wants with me, and I must find out right away." [289]

Then an extreme event occurred. From under God's golden throne "an enormous turd falls upon the sparkling new roof, shatters it, and breaks the walls of the cathedral asunder." [290] This blasphemous oneiric event was profoundly liberating. "Instead of the expected damnation, grace had come upon me," Jung recalled, "and with it an unutterable bliss such as I had never known." [291] It was a bliss of liberation from his father's "grace-less" religiosity, a gift of freedom from the earthly parent in the name of the true Heavenly Father. "I had experienced a dark and terrible secret," Jung remembered. "As a result, I had the feeling that I was either outlawed or elect, accursed or blessed."

Jung's turd-in-the-cathedral dream, which likely was derived from the religious revelations that came to Martin Luther while he sitting on the toilet, sprang from what he later called his Shadow. The Shadow is one of the archetypes that make up the Jungian structure of the "collective unconscious," that architecture of supposedly primordial images that every human being inherits, no matter what his culture or conditioning. The Shadow is the shelter of the instincts, the home of inspiration, man's primal mansion shared with all creation.

The beast in us has a powerful purpose, Jung said: to drive men out of the confining structures of stability into the open field of fertile uncertainty. The cathedral of civilization has to be violently defiled by the turd of instinctive life if it is to release man's power to act out of his most fertile intuitions.

*     *     *

Intuitive distinctions between the destructive and creative possibilities of violence are crucial in the adult arena of personal relationships. Here a clear sense of the characters of the people involved and the particularities of their situation is essential. Only then can an appropriate response to the actual context make violence valid.

A verbally furious quarrel between spouses or lovers, or between an employee and his boss, is liberating if it blows open an intolerable situation and brings fresh perspectives to the relationship. But if it goes too far and leaves too many emotional or physical bruises, it becomes destructive. Even then, however, the participants may usefully discover in the outburst that they really can't live or work together, and that the strain of sustaining an unworkable interaction is draining their energies and diminishing their spirits.

Indeed, the chain of events leading to an act of interpersonal violence may be so long and complicated no one but an accomplished novelist or skilled psychotherapist could unravel its sequence. Only a conscious grasp or unconscious intuition of those events can help the people involved judge whether the level of violence used was appropriate, and therefore essentially life-affirming. In some dramatic contexts violence may well be an expression of feelings that can't seem to manifest themselves in gentler ways because of the logjam of old hurts, buried resentments and ingrained bad attitudes. In such cases, violence is truly Kafka's axe for the frozen sea within us.

Many marriage counselors and psychologists know that an outburst of harsh emotions can burst the boil of a couple's psychosexual suppression, and begin the process of healing. Erikson himself linked the lack of intimacy in a marriage to an unwillingness to engage in marital combat, and George Bach and Peter Wyden of the Institute of Group Psychotherapy in Beverly Hills, California, believe that couples who master the art of battle with an "intimate enemy" can improve everything from emotional etiquette to sex, and relieve the pressure of harbored hostilities. Such couples, "feel less vulnerable and more loving toward each other because they are protected by an umbrella of reasonable standards for what is fair and foul in the relationship. Perhaps best of all, they are liberated to be themselves." [292]

The connection between love and violence was noted by biologist Konrad Lorenz. Speaking of animal bonding behavior, Lorenz said: "Among birds, the most aggressive representatives of any group are also the staunchest friends, and the same applies to mammals. To the best of our knowledge, bond behavior does not exist except in aggressive organisms." [293] This certainly will not be news to students of human nature, Lorenz commented. "The wisdom of old proverbs as well as that of Sigmund Freud has known for a very long time how closely human aggression and human love are bound together." In a famous passage in *Civilization And Its Discontents*, Freud wrote that "Men are not gentle creatures who want to be loved. They are, on the contrary, creatures among whose instinctual endowments is to be reckoned a powerful share of aggressiveness." [294] Following Freud and Lorenz, family counselor Israel W. Charny remarked that "It is fantastic to see that only among those animals who show significant aggression within their species does there also evolve a love bonding; that without hating-killing there is no emerging counterpoint of loving." [295]

A mythological tale from third millennium Sumer, one of the oldest on record, reveals the primal connection between violence and love. The legend concerns the goddess Inanna and her lover, the shepherd, Dumuzi. "I, in joy I walk! My beloved, my man of the heart," [296] Inanna exclaims at first. However, in the same breath she warns her lover that her love carries a fatal cost. "You have touched your mouth to mine, you have pressed your lips to my head, that is why you have been decreed an evil fate." Later, to escape the Underworld to which her restless nature has brought her, she offers Dumuzi up as a sacrifice to the dark powers. "She fixed an eye upon him: the eye of death!" and tells the demons to carry him away.

The Greek love goddess Aphrodite, like Inanna, and her Assyrian and Babylonian counterparts, Astarte and Ishtar, fuses passion and fierceness in her copious bosom. Aphrodite regularly cuckolds her husband, the ironsmith Hephaistos, with Ares, the savage god of war. Perhaps the love goddess simply enjoyed submitting to Ares's barbarous virility, the charge of his male violence. "It is not in giving life but in risking life that man is raised above the animal; that is why superiority has been accorded in humanity not to the sex that brings forth but to that which kills," [297] Simone de Beauvoir sardonically remarked.

Cupid is as much a god of war as of love, Ovid said; "Every lover is a warrior, and Cupid has his camps." [298] *The Kamasutra*, the ancient Hindu manual of lovemaking, describes passion as something like a vigorous quarrel. Carried away by passion, lovers may strike each other on the back, shoulders, head, or between the breasts. They may utter cries, thundering, cooing and weeping, "expressive of prohibition, sufficiency, desire of liberation, pain or praise," [299] and scratch, bite, bruise, suck and squeeze one another to intensify their pleasure. "Apply the *lingam* (penis) to the *yoni* (vagina) as it were with a blow," one instruction orders. "Clasp your lover's body with force, manipulate and pull the *yoni* open like a flower; kiss, pinch softly and rub the woman's nipple with thumb and forefinger." [300] Vatsyayana, the supposed author of the *Kamasutra*, specified eight different varieties of marks to be made by a lover's nails upon the body of his partner.

In the mystic sexual cult of Tantra, Indian Hinduism and Buddhism lay out a different route to nirvana than the psychic annihilation of desire inherent in Mahayana, or mainstream Buddhism. Tantra is allied with Vajrayana Buddhism, the so-called "thunderbolt vehicle," which uses magical practices to crack the spiritual barrier that blocks the believer from nirvana. Tantric goddesses are cast as lightning conductors, shooting electrical energy straight at the World Soul, the principle of universal unity. The adept, male or female, comes to a spiritual, not a physical climax by converting unreleased semen into a magical essence charged with the potency of a thunderbolt.

The thunderbolt as a sexual metaphor is continued in the French phrase, *coup de foudre*, used to describe the sensation of being struck by the lightning of love at first sight. This is the bolt that starts a fire, Denis de Rougemont remarked, and burns away the reticence separating potential lovers. Recounting an inopportune yet overwhelming *coup de foudre* that struck him and the wife of his host during a visit to Budapest in 1933, De Rougemont recalled their secretive lovemaking as a dizziness and a delirium, an ecstasy likened to "heat lightning in a stormy heart." [301]

"*Orgastic potency is the capacity to surrender to the flow of biological energy,*" [302] Wilhelm Reich italicized in *The Function of the Orgasm.* Such surrender involves "*the capacity to discharge completely the damned-up sexual excitation through involuntary, pleasurable convulsions of the body.*" [303] A young American woman Reich treated in the 1920s in Vienna was beset by an asthma attack every time her husband tried to make love to her. "Unconsciously, she suffered from strong impulses to bite and suck," [304] Reich diagnosed, and so experienced a choking sensation in her throat in erotic situations. He claimed to cure her by transferring her excitation from her throat to her vagina.

In Reich's view, the dynamic tension between sexuality and violence finds some marvelously devious emotional byways. The Victorian poet Algernon Charles Swinburne, for instance, found that being the victim of a beautiful woman's furious rage turned his knees to jelly. His cruel Dolores created a scenario in which "Pain melted in tears, and was pleasure; Death tingled with blood, and was life." [305] The nineteenth century Viennese novelist Ritter Leopold von Sacher-Masoch imagined a Venus in furs with icy green eyes, who whipped her eager "great mastiff." [306]

So long as it remains play-acting, masochism and its mirror image, sadism, is merely playful. A brisk flagellation can be fun, if it is governed by the desire and the tolerance of the participants. But flagellation requires "great delicacy and a certain *savoir faire,*" [307] suggested one of its modern celebrants.

And an inventive imagination. The famous, or notorious, "Berkley Horse," named for a popular London whoremistress, was a hilarious parody of riding to hounds. The gentleman, tied to the wood and leather contraption so that only his face and genitals poked through, was whipped from behind by one tart while another, half-naked, stroked his cock and balls from the front. The mock-horsemen were so delighted by their gallop that they returned to remount again and again, making Theresa Berkley a rich woman.

\*   \*   \*

A striking version of the tonic effect of violence in loving is presented in Edward Albee's 1961 play, *Who's Afraid of Virginia Woolf.* The drama features George and Martha, a contentious pair, who attack each other with a no-holds-barred ferocity, both emotional and physical. "Pansies! Rosemary! Violence! My wedding bouquet!" [308] Martha exclaims, when George brings her a mocking posy of stolen flowers. Later, George grabs his wife by the throat in a fury and threatens to kill her.

In their almost ritualized rage, George and Martha are passionately attached. Their turbulent feelings for each other reflect Fromm's perceptive remark that all passions are an attempt to make sense of one's life; and violence, along with love, is a crucial part of that endeavor. George and Martha know this in their bones, and as the action plays out they are led to reaffirm just how much they really mean to each other.

The brave, desperate couple test each other's calibre in the white heat of loving and its surrounding glow of sadness, need, and fury. Although their verbal and physical furies are shocking, Albee subtly balances such excesses against the depths of hurt and love that are their context. Every relationship is a power struggle, a battle to compel the other person to surrender his or her personality in favor of one's own, and in the end victory and defeat are much the same.

The complex and spirited intensity crackling between George and Martha is contrasted with the bland but cruel antagonisms of the younger couple they invite for a late-night drink. It is George and Martha's shared emotional courage, their willingness to risk everything, that tempers their affection, and the very force of their feelings validates their ferocities. However, if the emotional connection between George and Martha were less profound, less truly felt, their mutual furies would be little but a crude assault.

At the close of a long and painful night Martha acknowledges their vibrant connection with a moving soliloquy: "George who is good to me, and whom I revile... Who can hold me, at night, so that it's warm, and whom I will bite so there's blood... Who has made the hideous, the hurting, the insulting mistake of loving me and must be punished for it." [309]

In his essay, *Violence and Love*, R.D. Laing succinctly stated the challenge presented in Albee's drama. "We have to begin by admitting and even accepting violence, rather than blindly destroying ourselves with it, and therewith we have to realize that we are as deeply afraid to live and to love as we are to die." [310]

# EPILOGUE
## beginning to rethink

The Victorians paid a heavy price for their willful blindness about sex. Refusing to recognize that by demonizing sexuality it perverted personal and public lives, Victorian society lapsed into a perilously schizoid condition, struggling to split erotic experience from the mainstream of human feeling. This divided state of mind reflected even deeper levels of emotional and moral disjunction, just as our muddled response to the phenomenon of violence mirrors the depth of our current confusions.

In a few generations we have come a long way from the Victorians' almost total denial of the positive vitalities of sex. From our more enlightened contemporary perspective, it is hard to understand why our forefathers were so uptight. Havelock Ellis's once shocking declaration that "sex, as it is woven into the whole texture of our man's or woman's body, is the pattern of all the processes of our life," [311] has since become a commonplace idea. If he were alive today, Ellis, recalling the closemindedness of his contemporaries, would be astonished at our sophistication in this regard.

That's not to say that sexual energies have been wholly tamed; nor have they been magically converted into a totally benign force. The destructive powers of sex are still very much with us, from the incidence of outright rape to the murkier commercial exploitation of erotic imagery and the more vicious forms of pornography. At the same time, our sexuality is now allowed a wide range of benign expression at every level of experience, from the personal to the public, and this evolution of attitudes has greatly enriched our lives.

Where violence is concerned, we are now poised at a moment similar to the one the Victorians faced regarding sexuality at the turn of the century. The many manifestations of crude violence in our time are signalling us to rethink our conventional responses, to consider ways in which we may integrate this original force into our culture in a more subtle and complex manner. To fail in this is to risk a continuing degradation in the quality of our societies.

To start with, we must confront the currently unthinkable question: Can violence possibly have a positive part to play in our society? If we tentatively answer "yes," a basic alteration in our attitude toward violence would begin to permeate our consciousness - a gradual shift from condemning violence outright to acknowledging its alternatively vital purposes.

Rather than considering violence as a monolithic pathology, we might learn to break it down into its complex components and examine the many different ways it manifests itself in our lives. In this endeavor we can call upon the historical precedents we seem to have forgotten; precedents which reveal that earlier cultures, back to the Stone Age, have acknowledged the vitality of violence in everything from worship to love, avoiding some of the futile and unsubtle reactions that confound us. By considering violence in its many modes, we could begin to think about its varied possibilities for good as well as ill.

Questions: How may we now counter the negative manifestations of violence that in this century have so drastically shaken our belief in our cultural credentials? How can we go forward and invent new strategies of transformation?

It may be that, at this point in our cultural history, we might consider formulating a coherent "metaphysic" of creative violence: a mental construct that would allow us to discriminate between the positive and negative manifestations of violence, and create the basis for a coherent way of responding to the challenges and opportunities of this powerful fact of life.

A metaphysic of creative violence might be based upon the following trinity of concepts:

*That violence, considered as an energy, force, or feeling, is a basic reality of our experience as human beings; a phenomenon charged with positive as well as negative potential.*

*That an open-minded consideration of the creative responses to violence, and the positive uses of violence, can clear the way to a deeper insight into the elements that drive us and structure our lives.*

*That the effect of any such positive response to violence must enhance the scope of human possibility.*

Let us begin to rethink our approach to the whole question of violence, hoping that along the way many dangerous distortions in human relationships may be modified, that many current social and cultural deformations can be repaired. And let us remember all the while that mankind's record in integrating and transforming violence is one of the crucial factors defining our humanity; no other force of nature has more profoundly shaped our societies and our souls.

# FOOTNOTES

## INTRODUCTION

1    On Violence, Harcourt, Brace and World, New York, 1970.
2    "Leda And The Swan," Collected Poems of W.B. Yeats, Macmillan, London, 1933. p.241.
3    Nietzsche: The Man and His Philosophy, trans. R.J. Hollingdale, Routledge & Kegan Paul, London, 1965, p.171.
4 Civilization and Its Discontents, tr. Joan Rioviere, ed. James Strachey, Hogarth Press, London, 1973.
5    London Magazine, January, 1971.
6    "Lineage," Crow, Harper & Row, New York, 1971.
7    King John, V.vii.49.
8    Holland, Camden's Britain.680.
9    Aeneid, I.948. (1697)
10    Joseph Andrews I.iv. (1742)
11    "Easter 1916," Collected Poems of W.B. Yeats, Macmillan, London, 1933. p.202.

## ONE: CREATIVE MURDER

12    A History of Religious Ideas, Volume One, p.72. tr. Willard Trask. University of Chicago Press, 1978.
13    Wesen und Ursprung der Religion: Die grossen

nichtchristlichen Religionen, G. Mensching, 1954, p.11,12.

14    Origins of the Sacred: The Ecstasies of Love and War, Dudley Young, St. Martin's Press, 1991. p.120.

15    Ibid.

16    Holy Sonnets, XIV.

17    Ibid.

18    Ecstatic Confessions, Martin Buber, ed. Paul Mendes-Flohr, tr. Esther Cameron, Harper and Row, 1985.

19    Ibid.

20    Ibid.

21    Ibid.

22    Ibid.

23    Ibid.

24    The Language of the Goddess, Harper & Row, San Francisco, 1989.

25    Diogenes Laertius, Lives of Eminent Philosophers, book IX, sec. 20.

26    Primitive Man as Philosopher, Paul Radin, Appleton and Co., New York and London, 1927.

27    A History of Religious Ideas, Volume One, tr. Willard Trask. University of Chicago Press, 1978.

28    Homo Necans: The Anthropology of Ancient Greek Sacrificial Ritual and Myth, Walter Burkert, tr. Peter Bing, UC Press, 1983. p.3.

29    Ibid. p.xiv.

30    Ibid. p.22.

31    The Scapegoat, tr. Yvonne Frecerro, Johns Hopkins, 1986. p.94.

32    Violence and the Sacred, tr. Yvonne Frecerro, Johns Hopkins, 1982.

33    Primitive Man as Philosopher, Paul Radin, D. Appleton and Co., New York and London, 1927.

34    Genesis, 22.17.

35    Revelation of St. John the Divine, 5:12.

36    Apologeticus, 50.

37    Early Greek Philosophers, Fragment 105, John Burnet, A.& C. Black Ltd., London, 1963, p.232,3.

38    Ibid.

39    Eternal Peace and Other Essays, Boston, 1914, p.12.

40    Imitatio Christi, Thomas a Kempis, Abingdon Press, Nashville, n.d.

41    Frida, Hayden Herrera, Harper & Row, New York, 1983, p.77.
42    A History of Religious Ideas, Volume One, tr. Willard Trask. University of Chicago Press, 1978.
43    A History of Ancient Mexico, trans. by Fanny R. Binder from the Spanish version of Carlos Maria Bustamente, Fisk University Press, 1932, pp.59-60.

TWO: KILLING ETERNITY

44    Job, 3:4,5.
45    Ibid, 7:17,18.
46    San Manuel Bueno, prologue, trans. J.E.C. Flitch, London, 1921, republished, Dover Editions, 1954.
47    The Tragic Sense of Life, trans. J.E.C. Flitch, London, 1921, republished, Dover Editions, 1954.
48    Joseph Conrad, Life and Letters, G. Jean-Aubry, Doubleday Page, p.226.
49    Letters of D.H.Lawrence, ed. James T. Boulton, Cambridge, 1979-93.
50    "Defence of Poetry," 1840.
51    The Vision of Tragedy, Richard B. Sewall, Yale, 1959, p.5.
52    Nietzsche: The Man and His Philosophy, R.J. Hollingdale, Routledge & Kegan Paul, London, 1965, p.101.
53    Quoted in, Reading Georges Bataille: Beyond the Gift, Michele H. Richman, John Hopkins, 1982. p.108.
54    The Divine Comedy: Inferno, Canto I., tr. Melville Best Anderson, Heritage Press, New York, 1944.
55    Ibid.
56    Ibid.
57    Doctor Faustus, 1.1.
58    Paul H. Kocher, intro. to "Doctor Faustus," Crofts Classics, New York, 1950.
59    King Lear, 3.2.
60    Ibid, 3.2.
61    Nietzsche: The Man and His Philosophy, R.J. Hollingdale, Routledge & Kegan Paul, London, 1965, p.101.
62    Lectures on Don Quixote, Harcourt, Brace and Jovanovich, San Diego, 1983.
63    A History of Religious Ideas, Mircea Eliade, Volume One, p.263. tr. Willard Trask. University of Chicago Press, 1978.

64      Don Quixote, trans. by Samuel Putnam, The Modern Library, New York, 1949, Part One, Chap. I., p.27.
65      The 120 Days of Sodom, trans. by Pieralessandro Casavini, Olympia Press, Paris, 1962. p.10.
66      Proverbs of Hell.
67      The Marquise of O--: And Other Stories, Criterion Books, 1960. tr. Martin Greenberg. p.251.
68      Ibid, p.253.
69      Ibid, p.266.
70      Ibid, Preface, trans. Francis Golffing, p.23.
71      Moby-Dick, Modern Library, 1992.
72      Ibid.
73      Nietzsche: The Man and His Philosophy, R.J. Hollingdale, Routledge & Kegan Paul, London, 1965, p.168.
74      Ibid, p.172.
75      Dostoievsky, Nicholas Berdyaev, tr. Donald Atwater, Sheed and Ward, London 1934.
76      The Brothers Karamazov, tr. Constance Garnett, Modern Library, 1945.
77      Ibid.
78      Ibid.
79      Heart of Darkness, Penguin, 1988. p.107.
80      Ibid, p.119.
81      Ibid, p.120.
82      Celan, Paul, Todesfuge, The Jewish Quarterly, Vol. 2, No.4. (8) Spring, 1995.
83      T.S Eliot, The Complete Poems and Plays, Harcourt, Brace and World, New York, 1971.
84      Ibid.
85      The Collected Plays of Albert Camus, Hamish Hamilton, London, 1963.
86      Death on the Installment Plan, tr. Ralph Mannheim, New Directions, New York, 1971.
87      Metamorphosis and Other Stories, tr. Joachim Neugroschel, Scribner, 1993.
88      The Art of the Novel, Grove Press, New York, 1986.
89      Antonin Artaud, "States of Mind: 1921-45," tr. Ruby Cohn, TDR, Winter 1963. p.44.
90      The Theatre and Its Double, tr. Mary Caroline Richards, Grove, 1958.

91   A Short Organum for the Theatre," from Sinn und Form, Potsdam, 1949.
92   Ibid.
93   The Voices of Silence, Andre Malraux, tr. Stuart Gilbert, Doubleday, New York, 1953.

THREE: THE MARRIAGE OF TERROR AND RAPTURE

94   Bhagavadgita, trans. by P. Lal, Orient Paperbacks, Delhi,  Sec. 2. p. 20.
95   Origins of the Sacred: The Ecstasies of Love and War, Dudley Young, St. Martin's Press, 1991. p.143.
96   Ibid. p.219.
97   Musical Thought in Ancient Greece, Edward A. Lippman, Columbia, 1964.
98   The Renaissance in Italy, J.A. Symonds, Methuen, London, 1922.
99   The Composer as Hero, Philippe A. Autexier, trans. Carey Lovelace, Abrams, New York, 1992.
100  Ibid.
101  Ibid.
102  Letters of Richard Wagner, The Borrell Collection, ed. John N. Book, Vienna House, New York, 1972.
103  The Rise of Opera," Robert Donington. Scribners, 1981.
104  Passion and Society, tr. Montgomery Belgion, Faber & Faber, London, 1956.
105  The Journals of Andre Gide, tr.& intro. Justin O'Brien, Knopf, 1947-51.
106  Nijinsky, Pavlova, Duncan: Three Lives in Dance, ed. Paul Magriel, Da Capo Press, New York, 1977.
107  Margaret Conkey of the University of California at Berkeley and Jean Clottes, science adviser to the French Ministry of Culture. Quoted in Newsweek, May 24, 1999.
108  Structural Anthropology, Basic Books, 1963, p.372.
109  The Complete Letters of Vincent Van Gogh, New York Graphic Society, 1958.
110  The Complete Letters of Vincent Van Gogh, New York Graphic Society, 1958.
111  The Crystal Chain Letters, ed. and tr. Iain Boyd White, MIT Press, 1985, p.20.

112   Leonardo on Painting: An Anthology of Writings, ed. Martin Kemp, sel. & tr. Martin Kemp and Margaret Walker, Yale, 1989.
113   The Voices of Silence, Andre Malraux, translated by Stuart Gilbert, Doubleday, New York, 1953.p.641.
114   Exiles & Emigres, Harry N. Abrams, New York, 1997. p...
115   Reflections on Sin, Pain, Hope and the True Way, Sec.29, The Basic Kafka, trans. by Erich Heller, Shocken Books Inc., New York, 1971.
116   Constructivist Architecture in the USSR, Anatole Kopp, Academy Editions, London, 1985.
117   Futurism, Carlene Tisdall and Angela Bozzolla, Oxford, 1978.
118   Man's Rage for Chaos: Biology, Behavior and the Arts,' Morse Peckham, Houghton Mifflin, Boston, 1966. p.314.

FOUR: VIOLENCE MADE VISIBLE

119   Hispano-Arabic Poetry, T. Monroe, Berkeley, 1975, p. 346.
120   The Alhambra, A Cycle of Studies on the Eleventh Century in Moorish Spain. Frederick Bargebuhr, Berlin, 1968, p.98.
121   Le Corbusier, Maurice Bessett, tr. Robin Kemball, Skira/Rizzoli, 1987.
122   The Complete Poetical Works of Percy Bysshe Shelley, Oxford, 1914. p.546.
123   The Thinking Reed, Macmillan, London, 1936.
124   Upon the Gardens of Epicurus, in "Miscellanea," II, London, 1690.
125   Gaudi, Ignasi de Sola-Morales, tr. Kenneth Lyon, Rizzoli, 1984.
126   Futurism, Carlene Tisdall & Angelo Bozzolla, Oxford, 1978.
127   Ibid.
128   Ibid.
129   The Crystal Chain Letters, ed. and tr. Iain Boyd White, MIT Press, 1985.
130   Constructivist Architecture in the USSR, Anatole Kopp, Academy Editions, London, 1985.
131   Erich Mendelsohn, tr. anon. Rizzoli, 1985, pp.11-14.
132   "Deconstructivist Architecture," Museum of Modern Art catalogue, Philip Johnson and Mark Wigley, 1988.
133   SITE, Rizzoli, 1989.
134   Paul Goldberger, New York Times, 8-16-75.

135   Houston Chronicle, 10-19-75.
136   Frank Gehry: Buildings and Projects, Rizzoli, 1985.
137   Ibid.
138   Coop Himmelblau, The Power of the City, Georg Buchner Verlag, Darmstadt, 1988.
139   Ibid.
140   Architecture Today, Charles Jencks, Abrams, New York, 1982, p.83.
141   Ibid.
142   Kindergarten Chats, Wittenborn Art Books, New York, 1947, p.202.
143   Ibid, p.206.
144   The 100 Mile City, Harcourt Brace, 1992. p.5.
145   Ibid. p.305.
146   S.M.L.XL, Monacelli Press Inc. 1995.

FIVE: RIGHTEOUS WARS, CREATIVE CONQUESTS, AND JUSTIFIED REBELLIONS

147   Freedom and Civilization, Roy Publishers, 1944.
148   Ibid.
149   Ibid.
150   Ibid.
151   The History of Warfare. John Keegan, Knopf, 1993. p237.
152   Primitive War: Its Practice and Concepts, (2nd edition)H.Turney-High, Columbia, SC, 1971, p.5
153   The History of Warfare. John Keegan, Knopf, 1993. p237.
154   The Decline and Fall of the Roman Empire, Modern Library, 1932.
155   Moral Essays, To Helvia on Consolation, 7,7.
156   Aeneid, 1.847.
157   Epistolae, Book 2,1, 156.
158   "The Social Function of War," Robert Park, American Journal of Sociology, XLVI (1941) pp.551-70.
159   The Anatomy of Human Destructiveness, Holt, Rhinehart and Winston, New York, 1973.
160   Ibid.
161   The Descent of Man, Heritage Press, New York, 1972.
162   Ibid.

163  Works, sel. and tr. Jack Lively, Macmillan, New York, 1965.
164  Social and Cultural Dynamics, Extending Horizon Books, Boston, 1957.
165  The Dawn Warriors: Man's Evolution Toward Peace, Robert Bigelow, Little Brown, 1969.
166  Ibid.
167  Great Destiny, ed. F.W.Heath, Putnam, 1965.
168  The Rights of War and Peace (Sentences, Book II, Dict.44, Q.2 [2])
169  Quoted in Arthur Waley, Three Ways of Thought in Ancient China, Garden City, New York. n.d. p.131.
170  Ibid.
171  The Honey and the Hemlock: Democracy and Paranoia in Ancient Athens and Modern America, Eli Sagan, Basic Books, 1993.
172  Anti-Duehring, 1878, tr. Foreign Languages Publishing House, Moscow, 1947.
173  The American Crisis, 5, March 21.
174  Letter to James Madison, January 30, 1787.
175  Democracy in America, tr. Henry Reeve, rev. Frances Bowen, ed. Phillips Bradley, Modern Library, 1945. pt. I, ch.18.
176  The French Revolution, Modern Library, n.d.
177  Ibid.
178  Frederick Douglass and the War Against Slavery, Evelyn Bennett, Millbrook Press, 1993.
179  Points of Rebellion, Random House, 1969.
180  Malcolm: The Life of a Man Who Changed Black America, by Bruce Perry, Station Hill Press, 1991.
181  Young India, in Selected Writings of Mahatma Ghandi, sel. Ronald Duncan, Beacon, Boston, 1951.
182  Moral Man and Immoral Society, Scribner, New York, 1932.
183  The Rebel, tr. Philip Thody, Hamish Hamilton, London, 1962.
184  "Critique of Violence," in Reflections: Essays, Aphorisms, Autobiographical Writings, tr. Edmund Jephcott, Schoken Books, New York, 1974. pp.286-288.
185  Ibid.
186  Ibid.
187  Laws 1.644-5.
188  The Behavioral Persuasion in Politics, Heinz Eulau, Random House, 1967.
189  Ibid.

190    The Machiavellians, John Day, New York, 1953. p.38.
191    The Renaissance in Italy, J.A. Symonds, Methuen, London, 1922.
192    The Prince, tr. Christian Gauss, New American Library, 1980, 7.p.137.
193    Ibid.
194    The Range of Reason, Scribner's, 1953, p.138.
195    St. Matthew, 28:18, The Holy Bible: King James Version, New American Library, New York, 1974.
196    Ibid, 10:35,36.
197    Ibid. 18:6,8,9.
198    Ibid. 18:7.
199    Origins of American Sociology, L.L.Bernard and Jessie Bernard, Russell and Russell, New York, 1965.
200    The Condition of the Working Class in England in 1844, Foreign Languages Publishing House, Moscow, 1962.
201    Marx, Robert Payne, W.H. Allen, London, 1968, p.71.

202    Karl Marx, The Early Texts, ed. D. McLellan, Oxford, 1971.
203    Capital, A Critique of Political Economy, Vol.I., Foreign Languages Publishing House, Moscow, 1962.
204    Ibid.
205    The Letters of Karl Marx, ed.& tr. Saul K. Padover, Prentice-Hall, 1979.
206    Friedrich Engels, A Biography, Gustave Mayer, tr. Gilbert and Helen Highet, Chapman & Hall, London, 1935,
207    Marx et Proudon, leurs rapports personnel, 1844-47, Pierre Haubtmann, Paris, Economie et Humanisme, 1947.
208    The Anaarchists, James Joll, Methuen, London, 1979.
209    Ibid.
210    Reflections on Violence, tr. T.E.Hulme, George Allen and Unwin, London, 1916.
211    Pursuit of the Millennium, Norman Cohn, London, 1957.
212    Ibid.
213    Carnets 1935-1942, tr. Philip Thody, Hamish Hamilton, London, 1963. p.47.

SIX: THE STRUGGLE IN THE CAGE

214    Journal, January 5, 1856.
215    Dombey and Son, J.M. Dent & Sons, London, 1931.
216    Ludwig Boltzmann, Man, Phyicist and Philosopher, Engelbert Broda, Ox Bow Press, 1983.
217    The New Atlantis, Cambridge, 1900, p.34.
218    The Protestant Ethic and the Spirit of Capitalism, The Free Press, 1947.
219    The Technological Society, tr. John Wilkinson, Knopf, 1965. pp. 5-22.
220    Claude Levi-Strauss, ch.4, tr. Rachel Phillips, Farrar, Straus and Giroux, New York, 1967.
221    Uncertainty: The Life and Science of Werner Heisenberg, David C. Cassidy, W.H.Freeman, New York, 1995.
222    The Particle Play: An Account of the Ultimate Constituents of Matter, W.H.Freeman, Oxford, 1979.
223    Princeton physicist John Archibald Wheeler, quoted in the Los Angeles Times, 11.16.99.
224    Quoted in Chaos: Making a New Science, James Gleick, Penguin, New York, 1987. p.68.
225    The Unity of Nature, Carl Friedrich von Weizsacker, tr. Francis J. Zucker, Farrar, Straus & Giroux, New York, 1980.
226    God and Golem, Inc., 1964.
227    Science in History, J.D. Bernal, Vol II. M.I.T. Press, 1965. pp. 384, 386, 408.
228    Le Discours de la Methode, (1637), I.
229    "Remarks on a Redefinition of Culture," from Science and Culture, ed. Gerald Holton, Houghton Mifflin, Boston, 1965. pp. 218-235)
230    Nicomachean Ethics, bk.I, ch.I.
231    Confessions of a Dirty Ballplayer, Johnny Sample with Fred J. Hamilton and Sonny Schwartz, Dial Press, New York, 1970.
232    Violence Every Sunday, Mike Holovak and Bill McSweeny, Coward McCann, New York, 1967.
233    Clifford Gertz, "Deep Play," Daedalus, Winter 1972. p.26.
234    Quoted by Normain Mailer, Life magazine, March 19, 1971.
235    Beyond the Ring: The Role of Boxing in American Society, University of Illinois Press, 1988. p.235.
236    The Selected Poems of Frederico Garcia Lorca, ed. Francisco

Garcia Lorca, New Directions, New York, 1955.
237   New York Times magazine, 10.31.71.
238   The Labyrinth of Solitude, ch. I, tr. Rachel Phillips, Farrar, Straus and Giroux, New York, 1950.
239   The Anatomy of Human Destructiveness, Holt, Rhinehart & Winston, New York, 1973.
240   "Remarks on a Redefinition of Culture," from Science and Culture, ed. Gerald Holton, Houghtom Mifflin, Boston, 1965. p.218.
241   Atlantic Monthly, February, 1997.
242   Time magazine, 10.14.96.
243   Leviathan, 1651, pt.I, ch.4.

SEVEN: DANGEROUS LOVING

244   Anti-Oedipus: Capitalism and Schizophrenia, Gilles Deleuze, & Felix Guattari, Viking, 1977. p.1, p.54.
245   Introduction to the work of Melanie Klein, Hanna Segal, Hogarth Press, London, 1973.
246   Ibid.
247   The Anatomy of Human Destructiveness, Holt, Rhinehart & Winston, New York, 1973. p.199.
248   The Complete Works of Tennyson, ed. W.J. Rolfe, Houghton Mifflin, 1898.
249   The Anatomy of Human Destructiveness, Holt, Rhinehart & Winston, New York, 1973.
250   The Politics of the Family and Other Essays, Pantheon, 1971.
251   Violence in the Family, ed. Suzanne K. Steinmetz & Murray A. Straus, Harper, New York, 1974.
252   Ibid.
253   The Politics of the Family and Other Essays, Pantheon, 1971.
254   Ibid.
255   Human Aggression: The Need for a Species-Specific Framework, printed in  War: The Anthropology of Armed Conflict and Agression, Natural History Press, New York, 1968.)
256   The Language and Thought of the Child, Routledge & Keegan Paul, London, 1959.
257   Ibid.
258   "Grim Fairy Tales and Gory Stories," in Essays, Patterns and

Perspectives, Oxford University Press, 1992, p.138.

259    Sendak, Maurice, quoted in the Los Angeles Times, 12.4.91.

260    Ibid. p.138.

261    Ibid, p.139.

262    The Complete Fairy Tales of the Brothers Grimm, trans. Jack Zipes, Bantam Books, 1987.

263    The Bloody Chamber and Other Stories, Victor Gollancz, London, 1979. p.9.

264    Ibid, p.21.

265    Ibid, p.22.

266    Ibid, p.48.

267    The Lore and Language of Schoolchildren, Iona and Peter Opie, Oxford, 1959.

268    Ibid.

269    Ibid.

270    Memories, Dreams, Reflections, Pantheon, New York, 1963.

271    Ibid.

272    The Complete Fairy Tales of the Brothers Grimm, trans. by Jack Zipes, Bantam Books, 1987. p.197.

273    Selected Poems of Anne Sexton, ed. D.W.Middlebrook and D.H.George, Houghton Mifflin, Boston, 1988.

274    The Uses of Enchantment, Vintage Books, 1989.

275    Ibid.

276    Ibid.

277    Rough Magic: A Biography of Sylvia Plath, Paul Alexander, Viking, New York, 1991.

_ The Divided Self, Tavistock, London.

279    Madness and Civilization, Michael Foucault, Tavistock, 1967.

280    Prey Into Hunter, Maurice Bloch, Cambridge, 1992, p.4.

281    Ibid, p.4.

282    Ibid, p.6.

283    Childhood and Society, Norton, New York, 1963.

284    Story of the Eye, tr. Joachim Neugroschel, City Lights Books, San Francisco, 1987, p.6.

285    Erotisme, 54.

286    William James: A Biography, A.G.Wilson, Viking, 1967.

287    The Varieties of Religious Experience, Modern Library, New York, 1929.

288    Ibid.

289    Memories, Dreams, Reflections, Pantheon, New York, 1963.

290   Ibid.
291   Ibid.
292   The Intimate Enemy, George P. Bach and Peter Wyden, Morrow, 1969.
293   On Aggression, Harcourt, New York, 1966.
294   Civilization And Its Discontents, tr. Joan Rioviere, ed. James Strachey, Hogarth, London, 1973.
295   Marital Love and Hate, Macmillan, New York, 1972.
296   A History of Religious Ideas, Mircea Eliade, Volume One, tr. Willard Trask, University of Chicago Press, p.65.
297   The Second Sex, tr. and ed. H.M.Parshley, Knopf, 1953.
298   Amores, I, ix,1.
299   Kamasutra, Vatsayana, Park Street Press, Rochester, Vermont, 1993.
300   Ibid.
301   Passion and Society, trans. Montgomery Belgion, Faber & Faber, London, 1956.
302   The Function of the Orgasm, tr. V.R.Carfagno, Farrar. Straus and Giroux, 1973.
303   Ibid.
304   Ibid.
305   "Dolores," The Works of Algernon Charles Swinburne, Philadelphia, n.d.
306   Venus in Furs, Sylvan Press, New York, 1947.
307   Anthropological Studies in Strange Sexual Practices, Iwan Bloch ("Dr. Duhren") AMS Press, New York, 1974.
308   Who's Afraid of Virginia Woolf? Atheneum, New York, 1973.
309   Ibid.
310   The Politics of the Family and other Essays, Pantheon, 1971.

EPILOGUE: BEGINNING TO RETHINK

311   Studies in the Psychology of Sex, Vo.1. Methuen, London, 1897.